YOUR CHILD
AND SEX

A Guide for Catholic Parents

Very Reverend Monsignor

GEORGE A. KELLY

Random House · New York

[1964]

NIHIL OBSTAT   Daniel V. Flynn, J.C.D.
                Censor Librorum

IMPRIMATUR   ✠ Francis Cardinal Spellman
                Archbishop of New York

The *nihil obstat* and *imprimatur* are official declarations that a book or pamphlet is free of doctrinal or moral error. No implication is contained therein that those who have granted the *nihil obstat* and *imprimatur* agree with the contents, opinions or statements expressed.

June 6, 1964

Dedicated to
ELLEN *and* JACK

FOREWORD

How To Use This Book

THIS book is intended to help you perform your task of teaching your child the facts he should know about sex, and of giving him the attitudes he needs to lead a healthy and morally integrated sexual life. This, therefore, is a how-to-do-it book.

It is divided into two sections. The first section tells you in a general way what your child will want to know, how he will learn about sex, and why from his earliest days he should regard it as an important and natural part of living. This section begins with the truth that he could no more lead a satisfying life in ignorance of the facts of sex than he could lead a normal life if he did not know where his food came from or if he remained ignorant of other everyday things around him.

The first section describes how you can implant the thought that your child's sexuality has been given to him by God for a specific purpose. It outlines basic principles you will find useful in putting your ideas across. It traces his development from infancy to adulthood and suggests how to train him in modesty, how to deal with the experimentation that young children engage in, and how to handle the other problems that will concern you as he discovers the many aspects of sex in the world. This section will also give you an idea of the questions he will ask and the general age level at which he will ask them.

The second section provides specific answers to these questions and elaborates on the verbal instruction you may wish to give your child. This section has been written to provide facts and wholesome attitudes regarding any points which are likely to arise. It is perhaps more extensive than you will need, since it is unlikely that your child will question you about all the subjects covered.

I do not propose that the answers in Part Two be given word for word, since your own spontaneity is an important factor in teaching this subject. But you will find here the basic facts which you can then put in your own words. Information honestly and sincerely given, even if poorly phrased, is probably of greater value than information which may be more accurate technically but which betrays the fact that it is "canned" and is not something the parent really understands or believes.

This book will best serve its purpose if you read it now, discuss points of particular interest with your husband or wife, and agree on a common approach in dealing with your child. It also would be well to prepare yourself now for problems and questions likely to arise in your child's next stage of development.

But do not put the book aside and forget it. Refer to it occasionally to refresh your own concepts. If you are asked a question about sex that you have not anticipated, after giving your answer you might consult the book to see whether your answer was factually correct, and whether you gave the impression you truly intended to convey. If not, you might prepare yourself for the time when the question arises again, as in most cases it will. If you read the book occasionally, you may gain new insights, find value in suggestions which had not struck home before, and also strengthen your convictions about the worth of certain courses of action. Your growth in parenthood will come from the periodic examining of your own beliefs and practices in the light of new experiences.

Discussing this material with your husband or wife will help you clarify your own thoughts. You will also find that advance consideration of subjects involved in your child's sex education will enable you to talk about them with self-assurance when the need to discuss them with him does arise.

G. A. K.

CONTENTS

Part Two

Part One

How Your Child Will Learn About Sex

A RECENT cartoon in a popular magazine showed a father suggesting to his teen-age son that they have a heart-to-heart talk on sex. The son answered, "Sure, Dad, what do you want to know?"

This little joke would not even have been funny a generation ago. Then, parents were not disposed to talk frankly about the facts of life to their children, who in turn acquired their knowledge of the subject everywhere but at home. And while many youngsters reared in such an environment picked up false and distorted ideas about sex, most of them achieved a reasonable adjustment in their own lives because they were intelligent and grew up in a wholesome family with brothers and sisters. Also, the community itself let the young enjoy their childhood and prodded them into maturity somewhat slowly.

But all this has changed. We laugh at the picture of a young son saying, "Sure, Dad, what do you want to know?" because it is so incongruous. Sons should not be able to give that kind of education to fathers, but it occurs to us quite readily that this *could* happen today. Television, for one thing, has made even the five-year-old an expert on "the birds and the bees." Newspapers and magazines are so saturated with sex that we find nine-and-ten-year-olds skilled in the wolf whistle. (Some people think this is cute, too!) We have mixed dancing classes for elementary-school children and basic courses in biology for everyone. And should a child somehow reach his teen years in blissful ignorance, we can be sure that some precocious chum will wise him up.

Is there any reason, therefore, to be surprised that Catholic parents want to cope effectively with these new conditions? It is they who turn out in large numbers at any parish meeting in which this topic of "Parents and the Sex Education of Children" is discussed. Most of our young couples are well educated and feel that they can do a better job than their own parents. They also know that in an age of open sexuality the needs of Christian children are different. And yet for all their self-assertiveness, they, like their forebears, consider themselves inadequate to the task of sex education.

Why is this so? Part of their insecurity has been handed down to them. Reluctance to discuss sex with children has been going on a long time, long before the Puritans got the idea that anything pleasurable must be sinful. And it is not easy for normally decent people to be completely relaxed about a matter that calls for modest and careful treatment. Then too, parents who have every right to be concerned about the conduct of their children do not know how this information will be used. Perhaps they unduly extend the childhood of their sons and daughters, but it is quite natural to be sad that the age of so-called innocence has ended.

THE IDEA THAT SEX IS NOT "NICE"

More importantly, however, the hesitancy of many parents is based upon the conviction that sex is not a nice subject. Their own fathers and mothers may have taught them to feel this way. Perhaps their neighborhood or school experience was not wholesome. Their own sexual life may have something to be desired, and so the more their youngsters find out about life elsewhere, the happier their parents seem to be.

We are not criticizing the normal modesty of Catholic parents which derives from sound religious principles. Sexuality is a powerful gift of God, and the Christian either learns to master it or else becomes its slave. The world always tends to be excessively preoccupied with the flesh and to indulge its satisfaction. Christ and the Church, on the other hand, uphold the beauty of virginity before marriage and chastity in marriage. Both require virtue and self-control.

It is the function of the Christian parent to bring the child to the point where he can relate wholesomely to a member of the opposite sex and yet use or not use his sexual powers within the framework of God's laws, and without injury to God's purposes. And this is no simple task. It calls for balance in the teaching—proper emphasis on the physical and the psychological as well as the emotional and the spiritual.

Unquestionably, the best school for this kind of training is the home in which husbands and wives adequately demonstrate their love for each other. After all, good sex education prepares people for loving each other with feeling as well as with thoughtfulness. And this cannot be acquired readily unless it is observed. In this kind of atmosphere the child learns that affection is good and that showing feeling is proper. He learns how to keep demonstrations of love within reasonable bounds, and when emotions must be subordinated to other considerations. This learning process ought not be unduly handicapped by a cultural heritage which emphasizes the wrong things. For example, if we could criticize our own parents it would not be for their lack of love but for their blind acceptance of the Victorian idea that the man who repressed his feeling was the most civilized person and the one who displayed feeling was the most uncouth.

YOUR CHILD'S RIGHT TO KNOW

There is one other important reason why your child should be taught about sex: He has a right to know as much as he can understand why God made him male or female and what manhood and womanhood really mean. Just as parents have an obligation to teach him what kinds of food to eat, what clothes to wear and safety precautions to take if he is to survive in the physical world, so he must have basic training in the nature of moral and social living, and this means in his proper sexual role. When we say that the primary purpose of marriage is the *procreation and education* of children, we mean complete education—not education in every area but sex.

When God with your help created the human being that is your child, He poured a human soul into a sexual mold. Each male or female child reflects God and is made to His Image and Likeness in a different way. It is your duty as a parent, using the best of your abilities, to help your child understand what he is to do with his powers by first helping him to appreciate what he is—a man or a woman. This kind of wisdom is difficult to impart or receive when a child is eighteen years of age. It must be given from your child's earliest days.

WHY NOT LET THE SCHOOLS DO THE JOB?

As a result of the reluctance of many parents to teach their youngsters the facts of life, institutions have tended to take over the job. When large numbers of children fail to learn in the home, schoolteachers and principals think that providing an education in this area is another function they should perform.

Supporting the current trend toward the teaching of sex outside the home is the fact that parents generally have been falling down as educators in all areas of life. For many years now, the home has become less and less the place where children are prepared for life.

A few generations ago, a boy had a chance to watch his father at work on the farm or in a small shop or factory near the home. By watching and doing, he was able to acquire skills he himself would need to provide for a family of his own when he grew up. The modern boy may never see his father at work, and the latter has no opportunity to show his lad how to do certain jobs which will help him earn a livelihood. A girl could watch and help her mother sew, bake and do dozens of household tasks. But the modern girl has little opportunity to see her mother performing such chores, because so many of them have been taken outside the home. Thus the idea that parents should be teachers has gradually lost ground.

Moreover, educators, psychologists and others for many years have been undermining the educative role of parents. Example: The mother who wants to prepare her child for elementary school often is advised to keep hands off. She is sometimes told that her child should not be taught (or in some cases even allowed) to read until the teacher decides he is ready for it. Other mothers are urged not to teach their children arithmetic, because the methods they know are outmoded and may retard the child rather than help him. With parents questioning their own ability to teach, with "authorities" telling parents not to teach their children, and with the natural reluctance of parents to talk about sex anyway, it is perhaps natural that this subject is being taken over more and more by schools.

We do not say that teachers should not discuss sex at all. The intimate relationships of men and women have been a vital factor in history—and we can no more ignore them than we can ignore the influence of religion upon mankind. Nor do we want teachers to disregard the social aspects of sex in modern life. For instance, a child cannot properly understand modern social conditions unless he understands the tremendous toll in disease and misery caused by sexual promiscuity. He cannot understand the problems of our society unless he knows something about the problems of the illegitimate child. Nor can he understand the fundamentals of mental illness unless he realizes that it often has its roots in the unwillingness of a father and mother to accept the responsibility of providing a good, loving home for the child that has resulted from their sexual act.

But this is not to say that teachers are best qualified to instruct children in the *personal* and *intimate* aspects of sex. First of all, because sex is such an intimate matter, it stands to reason that the best way to instruct a youngster in it is to do so intimately—in a straightforward, person-to-person fashion. Every youngster reacts differently, and has deeply developed individualistic attitudes. Youngsters must be taught differently, and by someone who knows these different attitudes.

A teacher, no matter how sensitive, cannot adjust her teaching to make it fully effective with a group of thirty or forty children. In such a group some can almost invariably be found who are deeply embarrassed by a discussion of the details of sex. Some may even mistakenly feel a sense of shame in listening to the discussion. Others may be overstimulated sexually, no matter how discreetly the teacher handles the subject.

WHY SEX IS SPECIAL

A person's proper attitude towards sex depends upon his believing that it is something very special. A religious child should believe that his sexuality is a precious gift given by God to carry on a sacred work—love and the procreation of human life. The idea that sex is sacred and special is not encouraged when children learn about it in the classroom in much the same way that they learn that Paris is the capital of France, or that two and two add up to four.

Even if sex instruction could be given effectively in school, however, the question remains: Who can say that a particular teacher is better qualified than a parent to give the kind of instruction the parent wants the child to have? If it is true that many parents feel embarrassed or believe themselves ill-equipped to discuss this subject, the same may be said of many teachers. Just as parents have bad attitudes, so do many teachers.

Moreover, the parents do not even have the assurance that the attitudes that will be imparted in public schools are ones they want for their children. In our pluralistic society, we have all shades of opinions concerning sex. It is even possible that a public school teacher might person-ally believe that sexual indulgence—in the form of mastur-bation or premarital relations—is perfectly acceptable be-havior. Some teachers may see no harm in experimentation among the unmarried that stops just this side of intercourse. Others may personally believe that a divorce is entirely within the rights of married persons who are dissatisfied with the sexual performance of their mates. Still others may hold personal viewpoints at the opposite extreme—they may think it entirely improper for a boy and girl to hold hands unless they are seriously thinking of being engaged. They may consider sex a "necessary evil."

It is highly unlikely that teachers could hide their own personal feelings from their pupils when they discussed the basic facts of life, even if they wanted to. Therefore, parents who rely upon the teacher to provide sex instructions are buying a pig in a poke. They do not know what attitudes will be conveyed to their youngsters.

But of one thing they may be sure. That is, that public school instruction will include no reference to religious values. Many people do not believe in God or that God has anything to say about how sexuality is used. Therefore the schools must seek a common denominator that does not offend anyone. The result is instruction better suited to a class of medical students—instruction that emphasizes sex as a meeting of organs, not of people, and as man's private preserve to the exclusion of God.

Technically, there may be nothing wrong with such instruction. The teacher may be entirely accurate in describing the physical nature of women and men, how the sex organs function and how they come together in coitus. But there will be no discussion of the intensely spiritual meaning of this act and perhaps less than there should be of the emotional meaning. No wonder that so many children exposed to such teaching come away with the feeling that the act of sex is entirely physical—exclusively an experience of the senses.

The idea that sex is only physical exercise without spiritual significance is perhaps more responsible than anything else for the current breakdown in morality the world over. When God's purposes are ignored, sex ceases to be a means of procreation and becomes simply another form of recreation.

Under such circumstances, sex education in schools from which God has been excluded tends more and more to be education for contraception. If young people believe that God has nothing to say about sexual life, it is only a short step to believing that there is no sin attached to enjoying sex under any or all conditions. And once a person decides that no sin is involved in sexual practices outside of marriage, the primary question becomes how to avoid the natural consequences of the act. So there is a great concern with the use of contraceptive techniques, lest intercourse cause an unwanted pregnancy.

Many teachers have indeed reported that pupils increasingly want to know about ways to prevent conception—and that sometimes the knowledge displayed by pupils on this subject exceeds that of the teachers. Today, it is not uncommon for high-school girls to begin taking contraceptive pills, sometimes even with their parents' consent, so that they can reduce the hazards of premarital sex indulgence to the minimum.

It can hardly be denied that modern young people have more knowledge about the functions of the male and female in the sexual act than at any time in our memory. Nor can it be denied that there is now more socially approved intercourse among the unmarried than at any time in Christian history. It follows, therefore, that a knowledge about the way that the sexual act is performed is no assurance that young people will be chaste.

Information about sex is not enough. Regardless of how much young people learn about the physical processes of sex, they will not apply this information in a moral way unless they also have proper attitudes about it. Youngsters refrain from sins against the Sixth Commandment only when they clearly understand why God gave them the power of passion and only when they respect its awe-inspiring dignity. As we have seen, the best place in which a young person can gain this understanding is in his own home. Therefore if you wish to be sure that your children develop good and wholesome attitudes and that they make a healthy, normal adjustment to sex as men and women, you will have to impart those attitudes yourself.

2

When certain unspoken questions have occurred to their minds, and are troubling their senses, it will be then your duty, the mothers to their daughters, the fathers to their sons, carefully and delicately to unveil the truth as far as it appears necessary to give. A prudent, thorough and Christian answer to those questions will set their minds at rest, if imparted by the lips of Christian parents, in the proper measure, and with the proper precautions. The revelation of the mysterious and marvelous laws of life will be received by them with reverence and gratitude and will enlighten their minds with far less danger than if they learned them haphazardly, from some unpleasant source, from secret conversations, or from clandestine reading.

—POPE PIUS XII

Eleven Principles of Sex Education To Guide You

VOLUMES have been written about parents and the sex education of their children. Some of these books have been so detailed and confusing that they have caused readers to throw up their hands and consider themselves hopelessly inadequate for the task. Other books are so overly simple that they tend to make parents think sex education can be handled in a few minutes on a rainy afternoon.

Each of these approaches is bad. The matter of sex involves not only the body of the child but also his mind and his soul. It cannot be treated lightly. On the other hand, neither is it too complicated or difficult for the average person to explain.

In teaching your child, you will find that certain general principles will enable you to do the job most effectively. Whether he is six or sixteen, if you apply the suggestions below (and you must determine for yourself when and how to make such applications) you will give him the facts he needs, and also values and habits to help him use these facts in fulfillment of God's Will and to his own best advantage.

1. *Make sure that your own attitudes are good and that you set a good example.* Your own basic attitudes, even those hidden in the deep recesses of your mind, will color your whole teaching.

Two mothers had almost exactly opposite ideas about sex. One mother blushed whenever her child questioned her about babies or any other aspect of procreation. The other mother listened to her child's question, then answered calmly and in a matter-of-fact way.

These mothers had one thing in common. Both taught their children about sex. Both gave their children impressions which would last for a long time. Without saying a word, the first mother taught her child that sex is a hush-hush subject, something difficult to talk about, and perhaps not very nice. The second mother taught her child that sex is a part of life, something which can be discussed openly because it is good and important.

A psychiatrist tells the story of a woman patient who

came to him because sexual relations with her husband were revolting and disgusting. Under his questioning she recalled that as a child she had once asked her mother a question about babies in the presence of company. The mother slapped her and then locked her in her room. Another time, she heard her mother and father arguing, probably about some intimate matter, and recalled that the mother called the father a beast. This patient had learned about sex from the mother just as surely as if the parent had sat down with the child and told her that a woman's relations with a man are unclean and repulsive. Is it any wonder that a girl brought up under these conditions would find it difficult to enjoy the intimacy of marriage? It would have been remarkable had she overcome this training.

Some modern parents, reacting strongly to the mistakes of an older generation, may make the opposite mistake. In fleeing from that secrecy that derived from Puritanism, their approach may be common, if not vulgar. They may throw their children into the sexual arena, much like the untrained swimmer is thrown into a deep pool, without regard for the readiness of the child or for the consequences. Because they regard the sexual experience as physical and biological, they train their children to see only this side of sex. They do not seem to know, if they care at all, that in discussing the sex education of children Pope Pius XII used the words care, delicacy, mystery, sacredness and reverence. This is the modern heresy: To make sex an earthy experience and nothing more.

2. *Your everyday conduct is the best teacher.* A teenage boy often goes on fishing trips with his father and some of his father's friends. The lad generally stays quietly on the sidelines, but nevertheless he hears the conversations of the older men. They have a supply of dirty stories and

frequently refer to the extramarital sexual activities of their friends in an approving way. Nothing is said to the boy directly, but no one can possibly doubt that this lesson has been deeply rooted in his soul. No pious lecture will completely offset the impression made by his father's participation in these sordid discussions.

Another young man grew up in a house where both parents walked through the rooms less than half-dressed, where immodesty was the rule, where there was no privacy in the bathroom or the bedroom, on the principle that exposure to these facts of life was good for him. He remembers that once when he was at a tender age his father and mother had sexual relations in the front room at an hour when they apparently but mistakenly thought the children were asleep. This kind of education is only slightly less pernicious than that given by a father who introduces a teen-age son to a house of prostitution or to the use of contraceptives.

The point is, therefore, if you wish your children to have good attitudes on sex, you must have them yourself.

"By their fruits you shall know them," said Our Blessed Lord. Attitudes spill over into behavior, and a parent's good example is worth, as the saying goes, a thousand words of preaching. This does not mean that any father or mother is ever a perfect model. Such would be too much to expect. But you must be conscious that your actions will not go unnoticed by the ever-curious child. Your opportunities to give good verbal instruction will be far fewer than the opportunities to set an example of a good sexual life by the day-to-day way you and your mate live with each other. For good sex education is only one part of good training in living.

One father and mother take great delight in each other's company. Whether it is a day at the beach, a picnic, a visit with friends or relatives, a party or dance, going to a theater or eating dinner out, it is obvious that this man and his wife enjoy being with each other. When they are home, they find interests to share. They can spend an hour or two every evening discussing current events, they agree on what television programs to look at and they share each other's interest in music.

When they are doing these things, what are they telling their children about sex? They are saying that the relationship between husband and wife is by no means merely a physical one, but that there can be a union of heart, mind and spirit. It is obvious that their pleasure in being with each other, in sharing each other's ideas and ideals, does not stop at the bedroom door.

A father and his twelve-and-a-half-year-old son attended a motion picture theater. At the box-office window, the father noticed that the price for children under twelve was half the price for adults. He told the cashier his son was eleven. Later the boy asked his father why he had lied. "They'd never know the difference," the father explained. "Why pay twice as much as I have to?" This father would not want his son to masturbate or to have intercourse before marriage. Yet the youngster doubtless will encounter situations in which "no one will ever know." At the theater box office, his father taught a principle which will be easy to follow.

A husband and wife have five children and a car that is eight years old. Occasionally their fourteen-year-old daughter wonders why they cannot get a new car. She points out that many of her friends' parents buy new models every two years or so. Her mother explains that many of the other fathers are working away from home evenings and week ends, and spend considerably less time with their children. "Daddy would rather spend his evenings at home playing and talking with his family, and doesn't mind driving an old car if he can do that," she says. These parents are teaching their children something about relative values in life and are saying, in effect, that to them a child is more precious than material luxuries. Their children will be influenced by these parents in deciding how many children they themselves should have, and their decision will affect their whole sexual relationships.

The husband who is courteous, kind and considerate to his wife throughout the day, whether they are at home or with relatives, friends or strangers, is giving a true demonstration of the kind of love without which the sex act loses most of its meaning. If he kisses his wife and visibly manifests his affection in other ways in front of his children, they will come to understand what friendship and love in marriage truly mean. The wife who shows a real interest in her husband's activities and shows by her actions that she regards him as a man among men, is creating an excellent atmosphere. Both express their genuine love for each other in a spiritual and emotional way and the children learn subtly. Sexual experience is meaningful only through dedicated love.

In some homes (few, fortunately) the husband and wife rarely exchange a civil word before their children. He growls at her and she nags at him. Their children grow up believing that this is how husbands and wives act—and that courtesy, kindness and selfless concern for the other's welfare are not necessary. When they place the act of sex in this overall framework, it is little more than a connection of bodies—in a very real sense, a meeting of strangers.

A child not only should see love manifested by his parents for each other, but also needs to know that he himself is loved. Only by receiving love is he able to feel it and to give it in return. Your child will know you love him by the tender way you hold him, the smiles you give him, the kindness in your voice when you speak to him. As he develops, he learns what love is by the interest you show in him, by the fact that you enjoy being with him and playing with him, by your appreciation of his accomplishments like crawling or walking for the first time. Throughout his childhood, your guidance in helping him to develop—in short, your manifestation that you really care enough to sacrifice your time and efforts on his behalf —is essential to give him the feeling that he is a worthy individual who is loved and wanted.

During crisis periods of his life—when he attends school for the first time, moves into a strange neighborhood where he must make new friends, during his adolescence when he experiences strange and frightening stirrings within himself—he should know you are standing with him, ready with your encouragement and support.

But it is not enough for parents to give love. They must also take it. They must allow their child to show his affection for them by the means they use to show affection for him. He should be encouraged to express his concern for them, to develop an awareness of their needs, to be willing to serve them just as they serve him.

Psychologists have taken a long, hard look at many of today's coddled kids whose parents do everything for them and expect nothing in return. They have concluded that such youngsters are not overprivileged at all, but are really underprivileged because they have been denied the chance to develop their capacity to serve others and, in the real sense of the word, to love. These children would be better prepared for life and marriage if they received less and were required to give more.

Are we drifting from the subject of sex education? Not at all, for only when a man and woman know what it means to love and to be loved are they ready to participate fully in the sexual union which is an act of love. Knowing that true love involves a union of mind, heart and soul, they will be able to reject the modern myth that the act of sex itself is love. They will have sex in its right perspective, for they will know that intercourse can have value for both partners only when there is a communion of spirit as well as flesh. Knowing this, they will be prepared to make a good and lasting adjustment to sex.

A good sexual adjustment is difficult, if not impossible, between persons who have never learned to give love. Such persons know only what it is to receive. Consequently, intercourse becomes a contest to determine which individual can wrest the greatest sensation from the act, and fulfillment of the partner assumes minor importance. Obviously, when each partner in the sex act is determined to get the most from it for self, someone is going to be the loser. A lasting, satisfying relationship for *both* persons is obviously impossible.

3. *Sex education is a job for both parents, and both parents must talk.* It takes two parents for procreation. Two parents are just as important for education. How important they are is indicated by the answer of an engaged young man from Staten Island who, when asked how his home life prepared him for the marriage he was about to enter, answered, "I refuse to answer on the grounds that I will incriminate my father and my mother."

Sometimes men live under the illusion that it is the mother's function to take care of matters like this. And the fact is that mothers are far more aware of the importance of this subject and do more than their husbands to meet their responsibilities. But the subject of sex is so highly colored by the person talking about it that unless both parents are involved with their children the training is bound to be imbalanced. A woman may believe she knows how a man thinks or feels, or vice versa. But no man or woman can ever speak expertly or with certainty save from the vantage point of his own needs and experience.

A young child, for example, should be able to ask questions of either his father or mother. Until he is seven or eight, at least, the idea that this is something he should talk about only to members of his own sex will not occur to him. If both parents answer his questions honestly and directly, he will learn to have confidence in both of them.

At some time or other, perhaps at the age of twelve, children tend to gravitate toward parents of the same sex when they look for new knowledge or new explanations. This reflects nothing more than the basic modesty of most civilized human beings. And the father and mother themselves will be more comfortable in dealing with their respective sons or daughters.

This general practice does not have to be observed with absolute rigidity when circumstances call for an exception. For example, a fifteen-year-old girl bought clothing that unduly exaggerated her female form. The mother told her the outfit was unbecoming, only to be told in turn that this was the new style. One evening, the girl's father took her aside and explained that this apparel would provoke stares and undue attention from boys on street corners. He also suggested that respectable boys from good families would be embarrassed to bring her to their homes. It was this down-to-earth manly advice that did the trick and persuaded her to return the bizarre garb.

Similarly, mothers are better than some fathers in discussing moral questions with teen-age sons.

All of this, of course, requires talk. A set of dos and don'ts will not suffice, certainly not in an age when reasoning counts for much. These conversations need not be staged or stuffy. Sometimes even the best-intentioned adults become tongue-tied because of the mistaken notion that they must mount a podium or give a classroom lecture. Or they try to be profound. The more natural and simple you are, the better. As you might struggle through an arithmetic lesson even if your knowledge is not perfect, you can effectively educate your child about sex once you decide this is your job too.

And for the husband or wife who must deal with this problem alone, usually because the spouse is absolutely unwilling to help, we can only recommend that they do the best they can, perhaps with occasional help from a teacher, priest, doctor or devoted friend.

4. *Let your child know that God created sex.* Experience tells us that if a child is to lead a chaste life, he needs more than mere information about how the sex organs work.

It is unlikely that anyone can have a truly respectful attitude toward sex unless he also respects the part it plays in the propagation of mankind. For example, the child who is taught that sex is the means God created to bring human life into existence, and that the union between a husband and wife is the method by which babies are conceived in the likeness of God Himself, will be able to understand better why these powers should not be taken lightly. He will realize why God has given us very clear ideas about how they should be used. He will realize that just as gold must be kept in a vault and constantly guarded from thieves, so too must the power to be a parent be protected.

Unless your child has the idea clearly in mind that God made sex for a sacred purpose and that its use must be carefully regulated, he will not have the basic point of view that is needed to resist the many temptations that the modern world throws up. As I have noted, this is one of the main reasons why we object to group discussions of sex which lack the basic point of reference that God is the Creator of it all.

Youngsters who learn about sex without learning of God's relationship to it are like a person who learns to operate an automobile but knows nothing about the rules of the road. Not knowing what society expects of him, he would drive on the wrong side of the street, blithely sail through stop signals, ride the wrong way on a one-way street, and probably soon involve himself in a serious crash. A driver who knew the rules, but had no idea why they were necessary, would be somewhat better off—but not much. He might know that he was supposed to stop at a stop signal but he might be sorely tempted to keep going if he thought there was no chance of being caught. Such a driver would make expediency his first consideration— and would operate on the theory that it was OK to violate the rules as long as one could get away with doing so.

But in referring your children to God, make sure that they consider Him a Loving Father and not a heavenly cop. They must understand that God wants them to act in certain ways because, having made them, He knows what will make them good people. They must look to Him as one Who is ever anxious to help us, Who will be there when we need Him, Who knows the weaknesses of our nature and like a good father will "forgive us our trespasses." Your children will want to observe God's laws out of love for Him, more than because of fear. But make them realize that God expects them to do their best and does not take kindly to their making little or no effort to be good. Even Our Blessed Lord got angry from time to time at people who had too many excuses for not doing the right thing.

It would be too much to expect that a boy or girl will never commit any offense in thought, word or deed against the Sixth Commandment. What must be avoided is the feeling of hopelessness and despair which young people sometimes feel after succumbing to the weaknesses of the flesh. They must feel that God is always there to pick them up so that they can try to do better—not that He no longer wants anything to do with them.

A child often derives his picture of God from his image of his earthly father. If his father is just and merciful, one who forgives mistakes when the child is sorry for them, the child can more easily visualize God as a just, merciful and forgiving Father.

5. *Sex education must be education in self-control.* Probably the best reason for educating your child about sex in your home is that it involves discipline—the mastery over self. Discipline cannot be taught in a classroom like geography or arithmetic. It must be instilled in the day-in, day-out routine of living.

Fundamentally, your child must learn to respect the laws of God and the rights of others, and this is something his parents must teach in his formative years. In a real sense, therefore, it may be said that a child needs to learn how to cope with his instincts long before he is aware of the existence of sex. His ability to deal in a decent way with his sexual instincts will be developed when he learns to deal with these other instincts.

In view of the times we live in, it is more important for parents to teach self-control to their children today than at any time in memory. For the world outside the home has become corrupt. Nobody will deny this. One need only walk the streets of a city to see sex flaunted from billboards and newsstands, or even remain at home to see it exploited on television, to realize that much of the traditional sacredness has gone out of the marital act.

Preparing your child for the secular world is now somewhat like getting ready to send an astronaut into outer space where conditions are drastically different from those existing on earth. To send the astronaut off with no protection but a bathing suit would not be much different from sending your child into the world without the benefit of your teaching and example, and to expect him to have a reverential attitude toward sex.

Before we send an astronaut into space, we prepare him physically and emotionally, and make sure that he will not panic in an emergency but will do what is expected of him regardless of the circumstances that develop. With such training, he does splendidly. He responds to all the challenges which are anticipated and even to some which arise unexpectedly. In effect, through his extensive preparation he is enabled to conquer the hostile environment. It is sad to relate, but nevertheless completely true, that Christian parents must prepare their children similarly before sending them out into the secular world.

When you place sex in its proper framework, your child is being trained not only for marriage and parenthood, but also for celibacy and the single life if that should be his vocation. This is so because sex is considered merely as an aspect of life—not as a thing apart. The child learns that a life involving friendship and love is possible without the act of sex. He learns that the capacity to love truly—to achieve a union of heart with another—is a more rewarding experience than the union of bodies. When chastity requires that he abstain from sex, his sense of deprivation will be minimized. For he will realize that the sexual act is but one of many manifestations of love, and that whenever his vocation, whatever it may be, requires him to forego this physical union, a higher order of spiritual and emotional love for mankind remains within his grasp.

Let us make no mistake: The essential by-product of all

good Christian sex education is self-control. The world says the passions of the flesh cannot be controlled. Christianity says they can and should be controlled. Early in life the child learns modesty. Later, the proper use of speech. Then his parents guide him in his reading and in his companions so that by the time he interests himself in the opposite sex, he already brings to this relationship a sense of his own dignity and an appreciation of the dignity of others. And when courtship takes place, as it does for most of God's creatures, the parents, secure in the knowledge of their son or daughter's character, can as their final gift lead that child to the disciplined love of another which makes for great marriages and great family life.

The alternative to self-control is indulgence, immorality, and sickness. And in the earlier years the choice is more the parent's than the child's.

6. *Make the education gradual rather than abrupt.* If you understand the various stages through which all children pass, you will be able to anticipate your own child's needs and teach him in a relaxed, confident way. For example, the infant in his crib may often feel his genitals in an experimental way. There is nothing wrong with this. In fact, there would be something wrong if he never did so, just as he would not be developing properly if he did not display any interest in the movement of his fingers, the working of his mouth, or cared not at all about exercising his legs.

After the child begins to talk, he expresses an interest in babies and wants to know where they come from. Often, he does not immediately grasp the significance of the fact that the baby grows inside the mother's body, but is more likely to think that a baby is made in a hospital. When he is four or five, he has a greater interest in how babies are conceived, how they develop in the mother's body, and how they are born.

In the following chapter, I will discuss the areas in which children express interest at various stages of their development. This information will help you in a general way, but you should always remember that your child is not a statistic—that even if 99 per cent of all children by the age of five have expressed some curiosity as to where babies come from, the fact that yours has not done so is the one factor you must consider.

It is unrealistic, and performs no service to the child, to try to fit him into a preconceived mold. He has his own particular rate of growth, intellectual as well as physical. He may not want to know where babies come from until he is seven, and your simple explanation that an infant grows inside the mother may satisfy his curiosity until he is twelve or even older. Just as you would not be unduly concerned if he did not walk until he was thirteen months old, even though the boy across the street walked at seven months, so too you should accept the fact that children ask about sex at their own speed. Here again is a reason why you yourself are your child's best teacher, for better than anyone else you know what his rate of development is.

Have confidence in your own ability to teach. Many parents hesitate to discuss sex with their children, because they think they would not do a good job, and might even give false information—like using the wrong name for a part of the body. The same parents probably would feel no reluctance when asked to explain why a man speaking in a television studio can be seen and heard in their living room, or why the sun shines in the daytime but is hidden from sight at night. In either case, their answers probably would not satisfy a scientist, but they are accurate enough in a general way. And it is this general idea, rather than the specific, minute details, that a child wants.

Children can tell almost instinctively when a parent is honestly striving to give them correct information. After they start at school, they realize that their parents do not always have the correct answers about geography, history or other subjects. They willingly forgive parents' mistakes and misinformation when it is sincerely given, but they resent it when a parent refuses to provide any help at all. A parent who displays a desire to be helpful and willingness to be frank will be of greater service to a child than one who has the technical information but does not wish to discuss the subject truthfully.

Too many parents look for the magical moment to teach. This "perfect time" may never come. Yet in the normal course of your child's life countless opportunities will be given to you. Your youngster may hear you talking about Aunt Jane, who is going to have a baby. He will notice that only married people have babies, and may ask why. He may see a young man and woman kissing in the park and may want to know if they are married. After he learns to read, he will see newspaper stories about sex crimes. When he is in high school, he may hear of classmates who have been sexually promiscuous. In these and countless other examples, you will have a chance to explain, discuss, and inculcate proper attitudes. The more such discussions take place in an informal way, the more effective your teaching will be.

You probably will have to repeat explanations several times, because your earlier instruction sailed completely over his head, or perhaps at earlier times he was not interested.

7. *Be patient with your child's questions.* Some parents act as though their children deliberately seek to embarrass them or to engage in smutty talk whenever they ask about sex. It is possible, of course, that a youngster who perceives his parent's embarrassment at a question dealing with this subject will ask the question over again, just to stir up some

excitement. In most cases, however, a child asks a question because he is honestly curious.

To him, an inquiry about where babies come from and how they are made is no different from a question about where the cereal on the breakfast table comes from, whether the milkman has a family, or why it is that you can flip a switch and fill a room with light.

Assuming your child's honest desire for information, you will not manifest shock at anything he says. Sometimes he may use words that would make a worldly man blush to his ears. If this happens, however, he does not really know that he is speaking forbidden words or asking forbidden questions. Be thankful that you have an opportunity to tell him that nice people do not use such words—and that he is not using such language in front of people who would not be as understanding as yourself.

8. *Always give straight answers.* A young father and mother were discussing the possible answers they should give their child if he asked how a baby was put into the mother's body. Many suggestions were made—none of them exactly true. Finally the father said, "Look, let's tell Jimmie the truth. In that way everybody will remember exactly what we told him."

Many parents persist in telling their offspring that the stork brings babies and in inventing fanciful stories to hide the fact that obviously pregnant relatives are going to become mothers. These deceptions may buy a little time for the parents, but the children obviously will learn the truth sooner or later. When they do, they may react something like this:

"Mommy and Daddy always told me the truth when I asked about where meat comes from, how bread is made, and what makes automobiles go by themselves. But they didn't tell the truth when I asked them about babies. There must be something wrong in talking about these things. Maybe having babies is something that grownups are ashamed about."

Words in themselves have no significance—it is only in the meanings we give them. Words or expressions which are perfectly good to use in polite society in one country or language may be obscene in another.

Our reactions to words depend entirely upon our training: We react as we have been taught to react. If you give your child the impression that words which accurately describe the sexual organs are indecent, he may have a difficult time ever using these words, even as an adult, without embarrassment. For this reason, you should teach the proper words and use them from the very beginning. The child who knows that the male sex organ is the penis, that the girl's organ is the vagina, and that water passed from the bladder is urine and not "wee-wee," will not have to unlearn one set of words and learn another when he is older, all the while wondering why his parents did not teach him the true names in the first place. Some mothers and fathers hesitate to use words like buttocks and bowel movement in front of their children—a throwback to their own childhoods. You can get over your embarrassment quickly if you just speak the word aloud a few times.

When you visit a doctor, notice that he has no self-consciousness in using the proper terms when talking about such matters. The reason is that the words have become second nature to him. He thinks no more of using the word sperm, for example, than he does of using the words soap and water. He is matter-of-fact, and he has become that way simply through speaking and hearing the words.

Your child will also form distant impressions from the way you answer his questions. Suppose a child asks, "How does the father's penis get into the mother's body?" His mother answers curtly, "In a special way. Now run upstairs this moment and wash your hands, or read a book, or play with your toys." He will get the message: This is a subject his mother wants to get rid of as quickly as possible. On the other hand, if she answers simply that God has made a place for the penis in mother's body, the chances are that he will be satisfied and up to the limit of his ability somewhat informed.

For every parent who brushes off a child's innocent questions, however, there may be another who feels required to give a complete, detailed and, to the child, probably boring answer to every inquiry. One eight-year-old boy was arguing with a friend about why boys and girls went to separate toilets at school. One boy said to the other, "Let's ask your mother." The second answered, "If I ask my mother, she'll take two hours to give me the answer."

Between the parent who virtually brushes off her child's questions and another who provides an encyclopedic response every time, the latter is preferable. At least the child knows that his mother cares enough to tell all he wants to know. However, it is better to answer each of your child's questions in a matter-of-fact way, giving him the information he seeks, but without sitting him down for a long lecture.

9. *Never punish for sins against the Sixth Commandment.* Once you accept the idea that your child is struggling against the weakness of his nature, you can more readily sympathize with what may seem to be his fumbling efforts towards self-control. Recalling your own childhood and adolescence, you probaby will remember the inner struggles you yourself experienced. Even when a young person falls in this area, it almost always results from weakness rather than malice. Rather than being punished, the child

should be helped up and encouraged to do better next time.

Most parents display reasonably good judgment in this area. Extreme cases do exist, however, and sometimes they lead straight to a psychiatrist's office. One case involved a college girl who froze whenever an important examination came upon her. When the most important examinations of her college career were held, she found herself unable even to move her right hand. Under questioning by the psychiatrist, it developed that she had had an extremely severe mother who had caught her, as a young child, touching her genitals on several occasions. Each time, the mother whipped her severely. When the child grew older, she could not overcome the thought that her hands were evil. In moments of emotional stress, her childhood experience returned to haunt her. Of course, cases like this do not occur where parents or guardians have any understanding of the true nature and needs of children.

Threats of God's punishment for sexual sin also should be avoided. Your child should know that a sin against the Sixth Commandment is a sin against God, Who is all good. But he should also firmly believe that God loves us and is always willing to forgive us for our sins. The idea of holding the threat of hell-fire and damnation over a child's head is therefore a false threat, because God is more interested in helping us reach eternal salvation in heaven than in consigning us to hell for an eternity.

What is more, threatening a child with hell does not even achieve the result intended. Let a child (or an adult, for that matter) believe that the gates of heaven will be shut to him once he has sinned and that there is little or no hope of getting back into God's good graces, and he will regard his struggle to do good and avoid evil as a futile effort. Once he does that, he may turn away from God entirely.

Picturing Our Heavenly Father as a vengeful God may achieve another result, also bad: The child may become so fearful of incurring His wrath that he thinks he may be causing offense even with ordinary acts and thoughts. This is the condition known as scrupulosity—one in which, for example, a youngster goes to Confession on Saturday afternoon, is subjected to a passing thought about sex in the evening, and concludes that he is unworthy to receive the Eucharist the next day.

Always remember that a firm but kind spirit does a better job of educating and directing children than does a spirit of vengeful punishment.

10. *Give your child information before he needs it.* Early in their lives, your children are likely to ask you questions. But it is possible that they may not. Later, for any one of perhaps a dozen reasons, they may decide that sex is one subject about which they should not talk to you. The reason may be a native shyness, or perhaps they discovered in talking with you, relatives, friends or teachers, that the subject causes a great deal of embarrassment or annoyance, and thus it is better to avoid it entirely.

At any rate, in addition to questions which children usually ask, there will be aspects of this subject which normally would not occur to them. For example, you will want to protect your child against the possibility that he may be enticed by strangers. You will also want to teach him precautions to take in public toilets and in the use of public drinking cups to avoid contracting disease. You will want to protect him against play which might involve the sexual organs. When a girl reaches the age when she can indulge actively in sex, she should be warned against boys or men who would seek to seduce her. Boys also should be warned against older boys or men who might befriend them with sin as their primary objective.

Always instruct your child well ahead of the time you think the information may be needed. Most parents find that it is necessary to repeat a message at least several times before the child fully understands what they are talking about. By the time he encounters the situation you have discussed, he will be prepared to act as you have suggested.

In applying this principle, it is well to remember the wise axiom, "Better one year too soon than one second too late."

11. *Encourage your child to receive the Sacraments often.* Frequent reception of Penance and the Holy Eucharist not only will strengthen his will to resist temptation, but will also be a means of restoring him to grace if he suffers setbacks in his attempts to cope with the power of his passion.

It is best to encourage sound spiritual habits in your children while they are young, and before they encounter actual sex temptations directly. The child who has been accustomed to weekly Communion and frequent Confession will be habituated to the idea of continuing these practices in adolescence. He will know from experience that they provide a cleansing action for his soul and the grace and determination to avoid sins in the future.

Encourage your child to frequent the Sacraments, but never force him to do so. Probably the best persuasion of all comes from your own example. A child who regularly goes to the altar with his parents on Sunday will have more reason to want to stay in the state of grace than one whose parents do not care whether they go or not.

At times your child will not wish to receive Communion. Perhaps he has accidentally eaten before Mass, or does not wish to receive for various other reasons. God has given him a free will and this is his privilege. Never try to probe deeply into his reasons for not receiving the Sacraments. You might ask him if he intends to receive, and accept the answer he gives. Never give any suggestion by word or look that you do not believe him.

In view of the conviction that a child's private life must be thoroughly respected, it is a mistake to create a situation in which he is forced to receive the Holy Eucharist or is made conspicuous by his failure to do so. It is wise to give him a chance to save face if he chooses not to receive. The purpose, of course, is to avoid placing pressure on him so that he may be tempted to receive Communion unworthily to avoid your criticism. This would seriously worsen his spiritual condition instead of improving it.

One mother, facing resistance from her seventeen-year-old son to the frequent reception of the Sacraments, was quite upset. He had argued that going every week did nothing for him. Rather than press him, she waited for the right moment.

After a family birthday party, the boy went out to empty the garbage and stopped long enough to compliment her on "that great meal." She had a brainstorm. Walking with him toward the back porch, she said, "Thanks, John. But remember that while we can afford roast beef banquets once in a while, it's the hamburgers and hot dogs that keep this family alive and healthy. And you might also remember that a great spiritual uplift from an occasional Holy Communion is a rare experience. You need more than that to keep your soul alive."

As the boy went to bed that night, he said, "I guess that is what Our Lord meant when He said, 'Unless you eat the flesh of the Son of Man and drink His blood, you cannot have life in you.' " He was at the altar rail next Sunday.

❦ 3 ❦

The family is the natural nursery and school where the man of tomorrow grows up and is formed.

—POPE PIUS XII

What Your Child Will Want To Know

YOU may have heard the story of the mother who took her six-year-old son to a doctor for a physical check-up. After making a thorough examination, the doctor assured the mother that the boy was growing normally. She then asked when would be a good time to begin instructing her child about sex.

The doctor thought a moment, then asked, "How old did you say he is?"

"He's six."

"Well, you'd better hurry. You're six years late already."

The story is told to illustrate the point that your child's sex education, like his education for life in general, begins the moment he draws his first breath.

THE FOUR STAGES OF CHILDHOOD

The development of your child from birth to adolescence may be divided into four stages:

1. The infant gathers his first and primitive impression of the world about him. He learns the sensations of sucking and touching. He is aware only of such basics as pleasure and pain.

2. He discovers the other parts of his body—the power of his hands, arms and legs, the functions of eating and relieving himself.

3. He moves outside himself, and becomes aware of things outside his private world. He becomes increasingly aware of other persons and begins to grasp ideas. He is no longer satisfied with the knowledge that things are. He now wants to know *why* they are and *where* they came from and *how* they were made. He begins to ask questions about all phases of life, sex included.

4. The age of formal learning. He is no longer a baby, nor yet an adolescent. Much of what he learns now comes from what he is told as well as from the example he is given. He accepts what he is told by parents and teachers almost without question. Never again will he be so receptive to your teaching.

FIRST IMPRESSIONS ARE IMPORTANT

The mind of the new-born babe is a blank upon which his experiences will be written. What he learns about all aspects of life, including sex, will come not only from the words he hears later in the home and classroom, and wherever he has contacts with human beings, but also in the impressions now made upon his memory before he understands a word.

Psychotherapists tell us that our memories of infancy and early childhood play a crucial role in determining what type of person we will become in later years. Although your child in his crib does not comprehend a word, he is sensitive to such things as a kind voice, a smiling face, a loving touch. When his mother gently holds him close to her, she gives the impression that he is loved and wanted. She not only gives him the sense of security he needs for his spiritual, emotional and even physical development; she is informing him that his relationship with another human being can be a gentle and loving one. Being loved, he is prepared to love. Nothing in sex education is more basic than that.

He does not know yet that there is a male sex and a female one. But it will gradually dawn on him that he is handled differently by some persons than by others. He may sense a strength in his father, a directness, a love that is not so soft as that which his mother gives him. A son's impressions of these people he will come to know as males will greatly influence his future, for if he is given confidence in his relations with men, he will find it easier to take his place in a man's world when he must do so.

Similarly, your infant daughter perhaps realizes only very dimly that women and men differ in the way they approach and handle her, and in the sense of security that their presence and attention give her. These early experiences may do no more than pass lightly over her consciousness, but with time they make a deeper and deeper impression. Long before she becomes consciously aware that there are men and women, her own little mind will have already formed impressions about sex differences which may remain with her for her lifetime. Thus, sex education begins at birth.

This is not to say that the mother picking up her child for the first time must be afraid of the effect she will have upon the little one's psyche. We have had too many parents who fear to do anything with their offspring lest they damage him for a lifetime. But knowing that you can influence your child from his earliest days should spur you to do what you would do in any event: To show him love, kindness and attention, and to show your deep and unending interest in him as a person with an individuality of his own. The child who begins life with the sense of security that comes from being held close to his parents, and from being treated with gentleness and kindness, is being conditioned to succeed in adulthood, for it is through the security he has in himself that he will accept the tasks he will be expected to perform, the sacrifices he will be expected to make, perhaps even the heroism he will be required to display, in adolescence, young manhood, and during the whole of his life.

During this first stage of being, your child will also gain strong impressions about sex and the sex organs. At this time, he is most acutely sensitive of pleasure and pain, especially as it is experienced in his physical functions. The child who feeds at his mother's breast comes to associate this act not only with the satisfying of his hunger, but also with warmth and love. This experience is significant. He is likely to regard breasts much more realistically than if he were not familiar with this experience. Among many moderns, of course, the female breast has become a sex symbol. It is thought to have more to do with the act of intercourse than with the act of feeding a baby, and this idea seems to stem mainly from the fact that to a large extent the breasts have ceased to be used for feeding.

A child's first awareness of his sexual organs comes when he urinates and defecates. He relieves himself entirely as a matter of instinct and of course has no control over himself. He does what comes naturally.

Psychiatrists tell us that the child takes pleasure from

these acts, just as he derives pleasure from other functions he indulges in, like feeding and sucking. It is good that he come to regard these activities with satisfaction, for he leaves no deep-seated needs lurking in his unconscious as he moves on to Stage Two.

HOW HE LEARNS TO KNOW HIMSELF

In the second stage of development, he begins to have a greater awareness of his other organs. This is an exploratory stage. It overlaps the first stage and extends to the age of one year or so. The things he can do with his body —kicking his feet, feeling his toes and perhaps placing them in his mouth, grasping and holding objects he reaches for—become interesting and amusing.

He discovers that he can kick and he will do it constantly, taking pleasure from this new-found power. He will enjoy using his muscles to turn over, to sit, and finally to stand. He will use his hands to reach for objects in front of him. He will do these things naturally, and no one need instruct him. Without any teaching, he will also crawl, reach, walk.

No parent would think of punishing a child for performing such activities. On the contrary, each development is greeted with enthusiasm and appreciation.

Your child's desire to learn about himself and his powers does not stop here. His sex organs are as strange to him as his nose, ears, eyes or mouth. They too require investigation. And the natural processes of urination and defecation are subjects about which he expresses a natural curiosity.

Body excrement may become a plaything. He may even pick up pieces of it, rub himself with it, place it in his mouth or smear his crib with it. Sometimes parents, reflecting their own upbringing as much as anything else, falsely regard such actions as morally bad. Of course the child knows nothing about good or evil and is only engaging in a natural act of exploration. The best a mother can do is to clean him and the crib, showing no more emotion than if she were feeding him, making up his crib or putting on his diaper. She may wish she did not have the job to do, but she can console herself with the thought that the baby will soon tire of this little game and move on to other interests like making mud pies. Some psychotherapists say, in fact, that when a child plays with mud he is satisfying a desire to play with excrement.

What you want to do is to avoid focusing your baby's interest on his penis or anus to a greater extent, and this focusing of interest would be precisely the result if you were to punish him, or to express disapproval of his actions.

WHEN SHOULD TOILET TRAINING BEGIN?

Most authorities now agree that a child should not receive toilet training at too early an age. He will learn to control his bladder and bowels in due time. So why worry about it? In this regard modern parents have something to learn from European parents of several generations ago, who expected their children to urinate or defecate in their diapers for several years, calmly cleaned them when necessary, and considered the matter as natural as eating or sleeping. They knew what science is now telling us—that you usually cannot teach a child to control his bowels and bladder until somewhere during his third year, and that to try to do it before then will place an undue strain upon both you and your child.

Wait until your youngster is about two and a half years old before introducing him to the training seat or urinal. Place him on the pot at regular times each day—perhaps after meals or at other times when he has a tendency to move his bowels. Make a kind of game of it and praise him warmly when he performs as you want him to. But do not show displeasure if he fails and soils his pants. A sound psychological principle is involved here: Success breeds success, and the child who is praised when he uses the toilet will be encouraged to do so habitually.

TOILET TRAINING AND SEX EDUCATION ARE CONNECTED

What you should avoid above all is building up in the child's mind that there is ever anything wrong about the completely natural functioning of his organs. But you should not worry too much that you will cause your child permanent harm by the way you handle his bowel training. Most parents have enough sense to realize that it is unwise to try to force their child into behavior patterns he is not ready for.

Occasionally we read reports from psychiatrists that adults who are unable to engage in normal sexual relations were taught by their parents in early infancy that anything having to do with their organs of elimination was evil. Because of the association between the organs of sex and the organs of elimination, these children also came to regard the sex organs themselves as evil. The effects of overly strict toilet training also are shown by adults who seem to be obsessed by a desire for perfection and cleanliness. They are the people who must wash their hands constantly, who cannot bear to see anything out of place in the home.

Like most examples from psychotherapists' case books, these cases constitute an extreme. And while parents should be aware of the dangers from overly severe attitudes toward toilet training, they should also realize that if they use a little good sense and patience, their child will learn to use the toilet properly in good time, will feel no sense of guilt when he moves his bowels or fails to move them, and will ultimately be able to reach a relationship with the opposite sex which will be well within normal.

HOW AWARENESS OF SEX BEGINS

In this stage of babyhood, your own child will see another baby and accept him, just as he accepts everything else he sees about him, without questioning his origin or how he was made. His curiosity is almost entirely about himself and the things he can touch. Insofar as sex education is concerned, he may sense that there is something special about his genitals. He may be able to rub his nose as long as he wishes, and his mother and father may watch approvingly and smile as he does it. But if he handles his genitals in the same way, they may move his hands away.

He also senses a different attitude of his mother about certain things in the crib. If he spills some food, picks it up and stuffs it into his mouth, probably nothing will happen. But if he tries to put things like excrement in his mouth, his mother stops him. Thus, he is being taught to make his first distinctions between what is tolerated and even encouraged, or what is discouraged and even forbidden. He must learn to make such distinctions all during his lifetime and it is always best to teach him in a firm yet gentle and kind way.

If your words have any effect upon your child of less than one year, it will be due less to what you say than to how you say it. The word No means nothing to an infant, but if it is accompanied by a scowl or other negative gesture, he will come to understand that you disapprove of what it is that he is doing. Children are more sensitive to expressions than many parents realize and they sometimes can detect feelings which we think we keep hidden simply because we do not talk about them. That is why it is important to correct your own attitudes, if necessary, so that you will not be in the position of feeling one way but acting as though you feel another way.

LEARNING HOW TO LOVE

In the third stage of development, from about the ages of one to five, the child steps out of his small and private world. In the words of the psychologists, he begins to relate to other people.

He shows affection for his parents. Until now he has been entirely on the receiving end of love. Now he begins to give it. He may run to his mother and hug and kiss her for no apparent reason. These spontaneous acts of affection should be encouraged because one of the most important factors in his achievement of maturity will be his ability to express himself emotionally. Sometimes one meets men and women who find it almost impossible to speak kindly and affectionately to others. If you looked into their backgrounds, you would find that almost invariably they were reared in homes where displays of affection were never encouraged or were actually discouraged.

At this stage, a child continues to broaden the scope of his activities. He plays with other children, even when his mother is not present. He has playmates of both sexes, and he begins to form likes and dislikes.

His parents continue to be the overwhelming influence in his life. They are the real law to him, and his primary concern is to do what they want. Sometimes, of course, his actions stemming from some needs of his own will conflict with what his parents want, but there is rarely a deliberate intention on his part to defy them.

HOW TO TEACH ABOUT GOD

You can now begin to give him the religious instruction which is the base of all our beliefs and practices, in the area of sex and all others. It is fundamental that you give your child a belief in God and God's goodness that will remain with him forever.

One of the primary reasons why people lead lives in violation of God's Commandments is that they do not fully accept the existence of God, or they are confused about what God wants of them. For example, those who deny God's existence or believe He does not care what we do, can find no reason why intercourse outside of marriage is a sin. They argue that intercourse is nobody's business but their own. It is impossible to convince them otherwise unless they first are made to understand that God exists and that He wants the act of marriage restricted only to the married. If you would have your children have a good and wholesome attitude toward sex, therefore, you must first make certain that they have an unquestioned faith in God.

Your toddler will see pictures of Jesus and the Blessed Mother; point out Baby Jesus to him. When he can understand, tell him that God made everybody and loves everybody, especially little children. Make God a part of his life as soon as you can. Teach him to say a simple prayer like "Dear God, please make me a good boy." Encourage him always to associate God with love.

As he grows older and understands better, you will have many opportunities to get across to him that God is the source of all life, that He made us all with a definite purpose in mind, and that He has firm ideas about how we should act. You can give this concept to your child when he asks where the moon comes from, and the sun, the stars and the sky. You can tell him that they were made by God to rotate and travel through space in a certain way, and that if they failed to do so, sooner or later there would be a terrible collision. When they ask where food comes from, you can point out that God saw to it that there would be plant food in the soil and provides sun and water so that grains, vegetables, trees and plants can grow.

A mother was removing the liver, heart and entrails of a chicken before putting it into the oven to roast. Her little girl watched attentively, and the mother took this opportunity to explain how God had placed the organs in the chicken in just the right way. The girl then asked if God made human beings the same way, and the mother explained that God gave her a mouth so that she could eat and nourish her body, gave her a tongue to speak with, feet to walk with, and other organs inside her body that would enable her to become a mother when she grew up.

By discussing sex in this way, the mother clearly established that God has made all things for good reasons, and that we must use the organs He gave us in the way that He intended.

DISCOVERY OF DIFFERENCES
BETWEEN THE SEXES

Between the ages of two and three, your child will probably have contacts with the children of neighbors, relatives or friends, or with classmates in nursery schools. He will inevitably be exposed to the opposite sex, and naturally will be curious about the fact that boys and girls are different.

There may even be a tendency to examine the different sex organs. Do not be alarmed at this, because children do not seek sex information at this stage in order to shock their parents or to be bad. At the same time, they should be told that this type of sex exploration should not be done. They should be discouraged in a calm but firm way. Your child may not be old enough to understand why he should not do those things, but the fact that you tell him not to do them will be enough to deter him.

You may have to face some embarrassing situations resulting from his discoveries. A mother of a three-year-old boy was entertaining a friend with a two-year-old girl and put the two children together in his room to play with his building blocks. Half an hour later the boy excitedly burst into the living room to tell his mother that the little girl did not have a penis.

At this time, boys and girls may also try different ways of urinating. Boys may sit down to do it, and girls may try to do it while standing. You might explain simply that boys and girls are expected to do this in different ways.

Two extremes should be avoided. One extreme is the ultraprogressive nursery school where four- and five-year olds are allowed to run around naked and to watch each other at the toilet. The other extreme is exemplified by the mother who found her three-year-old daughter showing her sex organs to a neighboring three-year-old boy and took the girl into the house, whipped her severely and placed her in a dark closet for five hours. This experience so terrified the child that she grew up in panic at the thought that she might be observed naked by a man. The story was narrated to a psychiatrist by the girl after she grew to womanhood and found herself unable to take any interest in sexual relations with her husband.

HAZARDS IN GAMES OF "DOCTOR AND NURSE"

When your child is three or four, you can expect that he will play games based upon his own limited experiences. These games often consist of imitating parents or other grownups. Children may play store, with one person buying and the other selling groceries. They may play "Mama, Daddy and Baby," in which they take various parts (and sometimes give realistic imitations of their parents' shortcomings). They may play at being doctors, nurses and patients. Sometimes the "doctor" or "nurse" examines the "patient," placing a stick in his mouth or rectum to "take his temperature." If the participants in this game are members of one-child families and have never seen disrobed members of the opposite sex before, the game will provide the added spice of observing what little boys or girls look like.

Games which involve disrobing are perfectly innocent in the minds of the players. Even today, however, some adults mistakenly believe otherwise. One woman saw some children playing in her yard. A little girl lay on the ground while a boy placed a stick in her rectum. The woman neglected to call the girl's mother because she did not want to tell her that her daughter, aged four, was a "hussy." Fortunately, the child was unhurt.

Playing "Doctor" or "Mama and Daddy" may be physically dangerous, particularly if the children insert sharp objects into body openings. Beyond that, they do no lasting damage unless parents stop them in such a forcible way that the children obtain an indelible impression that something evil is associated with the bodily organs. However, you should warn your child against placing sticks, pencils or other things in the body openings, just as you would warn him against lighting matches or playing in the street.

THE GIRL WHO WANTS TO BE A BOY

A little girl may sometimes think she has been cheated because she does not have a penis as boys do. When she sees that boys can urinate more easily, she also may get this impression. Later in life, if boys are given more freedom than she—permitted to go places forbidden to her, allowed to play sports and engage in other activities which she is told girls don't play—and if in the family she finds herself the one girl among brothers who have a good time by themselves, she may grow up disappointed that she herself was not born a boy. If this attitude is developed over a long period, she may, to a greater or lesser degree, even reject her own sex.

Sometime, your daughter will probably ask why she does not have a penis. You might explain that God gave boys certain organs so that they could be fathers, and gave girls similar organs inside their bodies so they could be mothers. You might also point out that women alone have the organs to have babies and that men are denied the wonderful privilege of motherhood.

In any event, try to make your daughter feel that while she is different from a boy, she has many advantages and privileges which boys lack. Also that mothers will have many special satisfactions—not only of having babies, but also of nursing them, caring for them while they are young, and of being close to them all their lives in a way that fathers do not know.

HOW TO TRAIN YOUR CHILD IN MODESTY

Until a child is three or so, he will show little understanding of the need for modesty. When he is younger than this, he will not be embarrassed at being seen naked by others, and if allowed to do so would even run about the streets without clothing. There seems little point in trying to teach modesty to a child before this time, because he probably would not know what you were talking about.

By the time he reaches his fourth birthday, however, he should be able to understand that he should not show himself to others. He is also psychologically ready for this teaching, because at this time he generally begins to display a marked awareness of his own individuality. This sense of self is shown in how he gives and withholds affection. If Mommy or Daddy have spoken to him harshly, he may pout and refuse them a hug or kiss. He may also withhold his kisses if they fail to give him something he wants. Of course, if the parents give in and let him use his affection as a weapon to get his own way, they are encouraging a pattern of behavior which will become increasingly difficult to cope with as he grows older.

As regards nudity, parents can set a good example. A child who often sees his parents nude may find it difficult to accept the fact that he should keep his own body clothed. He may be unable to draw a distinction between his parents and other adults. So the best thing is for parents to avoid appearing naked, when possible, before children older than two or three years.

Here again, a moderate approach is best. While a mother or father should not deliberately appear nude before their children if they can easily avoid it, they should not go to the other extreme. For example, if a child rushes into the bathroom while her mother is taking a bath, the mother should treat the matter calmly, telling the child that it is not a good idea to burst in on either bedroom or bathroom and that it is always better to knock first because people sometimes want to be alone.

By the time your child is four years old, he will know that he should not do certain things. Until he is old enough to understand spoken words, he will understand only from your actions. For example, if he were crawling on the floor and tried to put a hatpin into an electric outlet, you would remove the pin and take him away from the outlet. You might have to do this several times before he realized that he must not play with electric outlets this way. Similarly, if he ran into the street alone, he would soon learn from your actions that he should not do so again. Until he learns to understand words, however, he will be unable to understand *why* he must not do certain things.

STIRRINGS OF SEXUAL INTEREST

At age four or so, children often are drawn to the parents of the opposite sex. Girls show a preference for the company of their fathers, and boys often feel more at home with their mothers.

This tendency to be drawn to the parent of the opposite sex is no reason for concern. It is probably a reflection of the child's primitive feeling for the opposite sex, a feeling which must exist if he is later to marry successfully.

There may even be signs of hostility toward the parent of the same sex. A little girl playing games with her father may become very annoyed when her mother enters the room or makes a comment which draws his attention away from her.

Later, however, this phase will pass. Girls will be found imitating their mothers while boys will strive to do what their fathers do, even to imitating Dad's mannerisms—the way he walks, folds his arms when he sits, laughs and so on.

THE QUESTIONS CHILDREN ASK

Few very young children think about where babies come from and what a person must do to get one. A young child may find it incomprehensible that babies grow inside of mothers. He has never known of such a thing. He knows only that people get things by buying them. They go to the store for groceries, to a stand for ice cream cones. If he learns that they go to a hospital for babies, he first thinks that infants are sold there like breakfast cereal sold at a store.

It may be a year or more—when your child is perhaps four or five—before he is able to ask specifically where babies come from. The answer that a baby comes from the mother's body may satisfy him or may not. Many children who hear this explanation shrug their shoulders, passing the information off as just one of the many things about the world they do not understand.

He probably will ask where babies come from a number of times and in several different ways. The same answer— that babies grow in their mothers' bodies—may have to be given eight or ten times before it sinks in. He may ask the question if a relative or neighbor has a new baby, if he sees a mother with a baby on a bus, or if he sees a picture of a baby in a newspaper or magazine or on television.

By the time he is four or five, however, he will accept the fact that a baby comes from his mother. Next he may ask how the baby gets out of the mother and exactly what happens when the baby is born. You might explain that when the baby is ready to be born, he moves through an opening in the mother's body and that a doctor helps him to come out. Again, your child may not understand what you are talking about and may repeat the question half a dozen times before he also accepts this fact.

Next, he may go a step further and ask more specific questions about the birth process. He may want to know, for example, how the baby got into the mother's body in the first place and how long he stays there before coming out. He may be satisfied with the simple answer that the baby's life begins when the father places the seed in the mother's body. He may ask what specific opening in the body the baby comes from. He may even ask to see the opening—a request which you should calmly turn down.

It is entirely possible that these simple facts—that the father and mother both join with God in the creation of a baby, that the baby grows for nine months in the mother's body and then comes out through an opening to be born—will be all that your young one will want to know about the birth process until he is a few years older.

The child at this stage accepts what his parents tell him without question—reason enough why parents should always tell him the truth. The myth that the stork brings babies probably originated with a parent's discovery in the distant past that her child would accept any explanation, and the story of the stork was a convenient way to keep the subject "safe." Parents who use this deceit do not realize, of course, that their children eventually will discover the truth and will seriously question why they were lied to about such an important matter.

Because your child now is so completely receptive of what is said, and so little inclined to question your wisdom, this is undoubtedly an ideal time to instill attitudes about life and sex which will remain with him for life. Actually, the attitudes you give him are more important than the facts. Remember that even if he cannot grasp much about how babies are born, it is more important that he believe that they are desirable, and that their mothers and fathers love them and are eager to take care of them. Your child *needs* this understanding for his own security, for he should know that he himself is loved and wanted, and that his coming brought joy to his parents.

LEARNING FROM BROTHERS AND SISTERS

In a large family with boys and girls of different ages, sex education to a certain extent takes care of itself. Since the average family does not have enough bathrooms to allow privacy for everyone, particularly during the morning rush hour, the sons soon learn that natural body functions can be performed without a sense of shame in the presence of other men. Sisters must share bathroom facilities and so come to consider ordinary activities, even bathing in front of others of the same sex, as natural.

At the same time, however, the children learn at early ages that there is a distinct difference between boys and girls. In observing their mother bathing younger children and in noticing that the older boys do not go to the bathroom with girls and vice versa, they do not have to have it spelled out that the sexes are not the same.

They also absorb the understanding that there are distinctive emotional and psychological differences. Seeing how girls enjoy activities like playing with dolls, while boys prefer rough-and-tumble activities, and noticing how their brothers and sisters respond differently to the rules laid down by their parents, they do not need to have too much explained to them in this regard. They know from experience.

The child without brothers and sisters may have to be told many things that the youngster in a large family learns through experience. For this reason, it is probably a good idea to encourage the only child to form friendships with little children of opposite sexes. If he can associate casually with the opposite sex in his early years, he will acquire some understanding of the characteristics of that sex—an understanding he must have in order to make a successful marriage.

HOW TO DEAL WITH DIRTY WORDS

At some time or other, your child will probably shock

you by repeating words which are obscene and vulgar, causing you to wonder where he ever heard them. Remember that he is merely repeating sounds he has heard, does not know their meaning, and does not realize that he is violating any taboos by uttering them. He may be repeating them because he enjoys their sound.

By the time a child is four, he has discovered that words have a power of their own. He may be intrigued by their sounds, repeating those which interest him over and over again. He enjoys words with a sharp, dramatic ring. Unfortunately, many obscene words in common usage fall into this category and once he hears them he may repeat them for the sounds alone. If he notices that his use of the words causes older people to prick up their ears, he may be tempted to use them over and over in order to gain attention.

Anyone old enough to pick up words is also old enough to understand that some words are not nice and should not be spoken. By this time, your child doubtless has absorbed the idea that some actions are permissible and others are not tolerated. If you correct this use of dirty words in much the same way as you call his attention to scratching himself publicly, picking his nose, or performing other unsuitable acts, he will understand that he should not speak the words, but his attention will not be drawn to them so forcibly that they will take on the attractiveness of the forbidden.

THE IMPORTANCE OF SELF-DENIAL

A mother also has many opportunities to educate her child to lead a Christian life, and a successful temporal life as well, by teaching him to deny himself simple pleasures. The time to begin is now, for one of the worst offenses that modern parents commit against their children is to do too much for them. Many children are never required to perform chores around the house, to help Mother set the table or clear up after meals, to care for their room, to rake the lawn or wash the car. They never learn the discipline of having to do things they do not want to do—and of doing without things they think they want.

As a result, many modern youngsters think they are entitled to anything they want just because they want it. They grow up without having any experience in doing what must be done regardless of their personal wishes in the matter. Instead of being privileged, they are actually underprivileged: They are denied the opportunity of developing self-discipline. Without it, they stand helpless against the urges of sexual temptation.

When you say No to your child, therefore, you are not necessarily being mean to him. You are teaching him that all of the worthwhile things of life come from making sacrifices and that little is accomplished by people who have been accustomed to give in to the first impulse that comes along.

All success comes from resisting temptations. The student who turns down the temptation to look at a television program or to play with friends when there is homework to be done is the one who will succeed at school. The man who applies himself to the problems of his job, resisting the urge to go out on the golf course every day, is the one who will succeed at his business or profession. The mother who resists the temptation to go off and have a good time for herself when her children at home require her care is the one who will do the best job of being a parent.

So it is with chastity. It is not achieved with a snap of the fingers. It must be worked for and sacrificed for. Your child must be able to say No to his impulses in order to achieve it. But it is unrealistic to expect him to say No to sexual temptation if he has been encouraged to say Yes to every other impulse that comes along.

CHILDHOOD'S "GOLDEN YEARS"

The fourth stage in your child's development, from the age of five or six until he enters adolescence, has sometimes been called the Golden Age of Childhood. There are relatively few crises in the normal child's life during this period, and by and large he appears to be making a reasonably good adjustment to his family and community. He accepts the teachings of his parents and the Church as a matter of course, and also more readily follows the rules you set for his conduct.

Now is an ideal time to teach—to give him good sex instruction and to instill religious and moral values. He is old enough to understand what you are talking about, yet young enough not to want to challenge your authority. You will have an opportunity to explain your basic philosophy of marriage, conception, birth, even death. If you talk to your eight-, nine-, and ten-year-old of the qualities it is important to look for in a marriage partner, you not only will find him in the most receptive frame of mind, but you will also be able to have wholesome ideas take root before he is exposed to opposite notions from others.

In one neighborhood, a wife with three small children took up with a married man who also had a family of small children. The philandering husband got his wife to divorce him, then encouraged the other woman to divorce her husband so that the two could marry. News of these goings-on was all over the neighborhood, and one nine-year-old remarked to his mother, "I really feel sorry for those three kids whose mother has run away and left them. Why do people do things like that, anyway?"

The situation gave the mother a chance to explain the sad consequences that result when people do not live up to the promises they make when they marry. At the end of the talk, the boy said, "I can see why divorce is wrong. When I get married, I'm going to make sure I'm marrying the right person. I wouldn't want my children to be stuck like that."

Be prepared to answer other questions about sex when your youngster begins to read the daily newspapers and to see television programs for the whole family. Even if his interest is primarily in the sports section or the amusement pages, he will occasionally read general news stories as well. In the press and on television he will be exposed to many subjects you might wish he did not know about. But he must learn about these things sometime, and it is better if he asks you about them. For instance, as a result of what he sees or reads he may want to know why unmarried people have babies, what the words "induced abortion" mean, what happens when a man rapes someone, what a homosexual is, and so on.

As your child approaches the age of reason, he will also ask thoughtful questions about sex—what happens to a baby inside the mother's body, how it gets food, how it grows, whether it has feeling, how big it gets, and so on. He may often ask how babies get started, and may wonder exactly what the father does. If he sees a pregnant woman, he will realize that she is going to have a baby.

He is now developing a strong sense of right and wrong, but he does not have a clear idea of where the lines are drawn as regards sex. One six-year-old anxiously asked his mother, "Will God be angry with me if I wet my pants?"

It is to be expected that these and similar questions will

be asked. If you can prepare yourself to reply in a calm, matter-of-fact way, your child most likely will be satisfied and will go on to other subjects without giving your answer much more thought.

There may be some sex experimentation. Boys and girls, left alone, may show their organs to each other and may even bring their organs together. For this reason, it is probably unwise to leave boys and girls of this age alone with each other for more than short periods of time. More common is the repeating of words used to describe toilet functions to the accompaniment of nervous giggling. The best way to handle this may be to tell your child calmly that he is acting like a baby and should grow up.

As a general rule, however, children from seven to twelve are not as curious about sex as you might imagine. It is still a somewhat remote subject to them, and they are often no more interested in the problems of dating and marriage than they are in the agricultural problems of Russia. Yet it would be incorrect to think that these years are insignificant from the point of view of the child's sex education. They are just as important as any others. They are a time when the boy begins to understand more fully about what it means to be a male, and a girl begins to comprehend what it means to be a female.

During these years, the child starts to develop the special interests of his sex, and he becomes more aware of its distinctive qualities. Before, it did not matter too much to him if some of his playmates were girls or if he was called a sissy when he played with them. But now he wants to play only with boys as a rule, and he develops an antipathy to girls which reaches a maximum intensity when he is ten or eleven. He will want nothing to do with them, will be embarrassed if seen with them, will blush at suggestions that a certain girl likes him.

Left to their own devices, children in this pre-adolescent period would not think of having dances, parties or dates with the opposite sex. Boys in particular want to be with boys, and while some girls are farther advanced than boys, they usually realize that their time has not yet come. Whenever there is dancing and dating among elementary-school children, almost invariably an overeager parent can be found in the background.

Early dating serves absolutely no useful purpose. The children are years removed from when they could seriously think of marriage, and dating among young people makes good sense only when marriage is a possibility. Even if dates are customary among elementary-school children, you would be wise to discourage your own youngsters from them. They will have time enough to date later, when they will be better equipped to handle the moral problems that dating and its natural development, going steady, involve.

During these years, your son will want to grow closer to his father. He will prefer to do things with Dad. His mother may have difficulty at times in getting him to run errands or do things around the house, but he will generally do quickly what his father tells him. In dozens of ways, he will make it apparent that he wants to develop his masculinity —to be a man.

At the same time, girls will show a definite preference for female company. Their interests are sharply divergent from those of boys. Brothers and sisters will seem to have little in common, and the fact that they are moving in opposite directions may underlie some of the arguments and disagreements between them.

Wise parents encourage their boys to move along these lines of greater masculinity and their girls to develop their femininity. They know that a man must not doubt that he can maintain a place among his own sex, if he is to lead a happy life. He must be sure of his own masculinity if he is to serve as a successful husband and as a model for his own boys.

Likewise, a girl with an abiding sense of her own femaleness is best equipped for any roles she will play in adult life. She can achieve this sense only by identifying herself closely with other females. In order to know that she herself is a woman, she must clearly understand how women think, feel and act.

While boys and girls in their pre-teen years seem to be concentrating on taking on the characteristics of their own sex, they are also picking up attitudes and information which will form a basic part of their adult attitude toward the other sex. They will watch their parents closely, observing how Dad expresses his affection for Mother, how he is sympathetic and helpful when she is ill, and how she bolsters him up when he feels low. When children see their parents together, they think that this is how fathers and mothers act—and this is how they themselves will tend to act if they become husbands and wives.

Even squabbles between father and mother have a value for the children. Youngsters should learn that a husband and wife should be courteous and considerate toward each other. But they should also learn that parents lack the perfection of saints, and that there sometimes will be strong differences of opinion and even spirited arguments. It probably is good for children to see some conflict between their parents occasionally, because they would be improperly trained if they themselves entered marriage expecting forty or fifty years of serene, uninterrupted smoothness. They need to know that at times every husband and wife see things differently and find it difficult, even impossible, to reconcile their viewpoints.

But if children learn that some disagreements between husband and wife are inevitable, they should also learn that respect—the basic, underlying foundations of mutual love—remains unshaken. If it is helpful for them to know that parents sometimes disagree firmly, it is even more helpful to know that parents always make up, and that in a true Christian home there is always a genuine spirit of forgiveness.

WHAT TO DO IF YOUR CHILD
ASKS NO QUESTIONS ABOUT SEX

As this brief timetable of your child's developing awareness indicates, sex education is no different from other types of education in that one thing slowly but surely leads to another. In using this chronology to get a general idea of what to expect from your child, remember that no two children are alike. While their awareness of the facts of life follows a general pattern of development, some children will be more advanced in some respects than others. For example, your twelve-year-old may have heard you explain years ago that babies come from their mothers' bodies and that fathers plant the seed. This explanation may satisfy his curiosity entirely, and other things about sex he reads, sees on television, or overhears may sail over his head. Another child of the same age may encounter the same references about sex and ask a hundred questions.

A child can get by with a small amount of information on this subject. He need only know enough to maintain his own chastity and to develop the attitude that there is nothing obscene about the sex act when it is performed in a moral way. It cannot be said too often that the information itself is secondary. What is more important is the attitude about it that you transmit.

If he does not ask the basic questions by this time, he should be told. A mother should take her daughter aside and tell her what she can expect with menstruation—how it begins and ends, and what it signifies. The girl must be told that she is entering the period when she could become a mother and that it is possible for unmarried people to have babies. You should warn her against any activities with boys involving sex, because once sexual desire is created it may be difficult to quell short of intercourse.

A mother's attitude about menstruation is important. Even if she herself has difficulties and severe pains during menstruation, she should try not to let her own exceptional experience color what she tells her daughter. A girl who expects menstruation to be fraught with pain will imagine terrors worse than anything experienced in reality. To a certain extent the mind can control matter, and the girl who expects menstruation to be nothing more than a period of minor annoyance will be likely to find that in reality it is just that.

A father should make sure that his son approaching adolescence knows at least the basic facts of life. Particularly, the father should explain that the boy's sex organs are growing so that he can become a father later, and that the boy can expect seed to be discharged in his sleep. Material that might be included in a mother's talk to her daughter and a father's talk to his son is contained in Part Two under the heading "Growing Up."

As long as the parents' attitudes are right and they keep open the lines of communication to their child, the amount of information above the basic minimum he may have at any particular time will be of secondary moment. The most important thing is that the child know that his sexual powers are a gift from God which must be used with reverence and gratitude.

ENCOURAGE THE EUCHARIST AS "FOOD FOR THE SOUL"

You will find, during your child's early life, that a life of chastity will be made easier through frequent reception of the Sacraments. As soon as he can understand, he should learn that God loves him and will always forgive any offense he truly regrets. Long before any question of sexual sin even enters his mind, encourage him to develop the habit of frequenting the Confessional in order to keep himself in the state of grace and to fortify himself against future temptations.

Also encourage him to receive the Eucharist as often as possible. He will be most influenced, of course, by his parents in this regard. If they go to the altar rail regularly, it will become a matter of course for him to do likewise, and if this pattern is acquired in pre-adolescence it will stand him in good stead when he enters the stress and strain of the teen years.

You can give your child a good idea of the value of the Eucharist by referring to it as necessary food for the soul. By the time he is seven, he doubtless realizes that certain foods are good for him because they build sound bodies and strong bones. If television commercials have done nothing else, they have made children aware of the importance of good food for strength and health.

STRANGE MEN AND YOUR CHILD

In every community of a few thousand persons or more, there probably can be found one or more men who might be termed peculiar. Perhaps the men are suffering from a kind of neurosis which makes them act in peculiar ways. But they may also be men who take a perverse delight in molesting little children.

Every mother who allows her boy or girl out on the street must face the possibility that some stranger may try to entice the child into some secluded place with the intention of doing harm. Despite the stories one occasionally reads in the newspapers, these possibilities are somewhat remote, but they do exist. Therefore, it is necessary for a mother to instruct her child and to take reasonable precautions concerning this danger.

You do not want to impress your child so intensely with the dangers of talking to men that he becomes fearful of everyone he meets. On the other hand, if he is allowed a certain freedom outside the home, he must also learn that he cannot trust everyone. When your child is old enough to understand, you might explain that some bad men stop little girls and boys on the street, sometimes offering candy or money, and sometimes trying to take the children some place where they can harm them. Instruct your child not to go anyplace with a strange man, never to take money, candy or other gifts from him, and never to get into an automobile with him. It may be necessary to repeat these warnings several times to make sure that your child fully understands. It is also a good idea to repeat it every few months or so.

If your child reports having been stopped by a stranger, you would do well to investigate. By checking into such matters, you may be able to prevent tragedies from striking elsewhere. One woman in Brooklyn, told that a man had approached her daughter, went into the street just in time to see another child enter the man's car. She was able to get the child from the car before the man drove off, and by noting the license plate was able to direct police to a man with a record of convictions for sexual offenses.

Your son also should be reminded from time to time of the risks involved in striking up friendships with those very much older than himself. It has been said that a large number of homosexuals have been introduced into this practice by older persons. Some try to get young boys to commit sins with them. They do it by pretending to be friendly and sometimes by even offering gifts of money, jewelry or other things.

Occasionally newspapers carry stories of brutal assaults which have been committed on children. Your own youngsters may read these tales. Always keeping in mind that you do not want to make them fearful of all strangers, you may find that these stories give you an opportunity to remind them of necessary precautions they should take.

❧ 4 ❧

Look about you at the crowd of children that de-
plorable negligence exposes to the dangers of bad
reading, of indecent shows, of unhealthy company, or
those that blind love rears in the immoderate love of
ease and frivolities, to the practical forgetfulness, if
not contempt, of the great moral laws: the duty
of prayer, the necessity of sacrifice and of victory over
the passions.

—POPE PIUS XII

Teen-agers and the
Years of Crisis

THE most challenging time for parents undoubtedly is a
child's adolescence—his teen years. Adolescence is one of
life's crisis periods. It marks the beginning of a child's active
sex life. Now, for the first time, he feels a positive urge to
relieve the sexual tensions building up inside his body. And
as he is developing physically and acquiring the capacity
to engage in sexual acts, he is also developing emotionally
and intellectually.

This is the period when a child begins to move away from his parents and to seek greater freedom. During these teen years, he becomes increasingly aware of his ability to do things for himself, and he often tends to resist his parents' efforts to tell him how to do them. Moreover, he begins to see himself as an adult, and he wants to take on the prerogatives of adulthood. He usually wants more privileges than his parents consider it wise to give him. Because he is striking out to establish his own identity independent of his parents and they seem to be frustrating him, he is likely to be quite rebellious at times.

When he rebels, his parents might well look outside the home for some of the explanation. True, it is during adolescence that their own chickens come home to roost. If you have consistently lived by a double standard—a strict one for your children and a more indulgent one for yourself—you should not be surprised if your offspring now look at you with a critical eye.

Even if you are as free of fault as it is possible to be, modern society will create problems for you. Your young are unlikely to revere a culture which has many features of decadence resulting from bad ideas and performances by adults. When violence and corruption pervade high places, one cannot expect future leaders to be impressed. And in a society which preaches freedom so often and so loudly, with little consideration for the law, order and responsibility which should accompany freedom, it is surprising to find as much obedience as there is in our homes.

TWO WRONG DIRECTIONS OF ADOLESCENCE

The adolescent is in the second major stage of his life. His parents and his faith, along with the standards they hold up to him, are undergoing scrutiny. If there is an imbalance between the proper authority of parents and the rightful freedom of children, the result will be either adolescent sheep ("Whatever mama wants, mama should get") or adolescent rebels ("The gall of my parents—denying me my civil rights!"). The normal teen-ager will not often act at either of these extremes. You can expect him to be compliant at times—but at other times he will try to use his nearby relatives as a punching bag.

For whatever reason, we are probably more aware today of the problems of adolescence than we have ever been. A generation ago, the fourteen- or fifteen-year-old was still regarded as a child. Even older teen-agers—the eighteen- and nineteen-year-olds—were subject to parents' firm control and given little freedom to think or act for themselves. Some moderns say these adolescents of earlier times were repressed and hampered in their normal development. This is a gross exageration. But to say that is not to deny that the "teen-age problem" has become a matter of public concern in recent years.

A generation ago, if difficulties arose in family living, the teen-ager was expected to adjust to the demands of his parents. Today, it often happens that the parents are expected to adjust to the teen-ager. It is no coincidence that books and magazine articles with titles like "How to Get Along with Your Teen-ager" are now widely circulated, and presumably widely read.

It has been said that teen-agers have become one of the nation's most effective pressure groups. For example, the financial pages report that through their allowances or earnings, they spend ten billion dollars every year. Advertisers striving to reach this market naturally cater to the desires of the young to be older than they really are. As a result, teen-agers are encouraged to splurge on "adult" merchandise—perhaps cosmetics their parents would not ordinarily want them to have, perhaps more daring dresses or bathing suits, perhaps provocative records, perhaps motion pictures with scenes their parents might not consider suitable for them. All in all, there are strong commercial reasons for giving teen-agers the impression that they know more about living than their parents want them to know.

THE FEAR OF BEING DIFFERENT

As anyone who has ever observed an elementary school graduating class can testify, growth rates of thirteen-, fourteen- and fifteen-year-olds are decidedly uneven. Since girls mature earlier than boys, it is not unusual to see a girl over five feet at one end of the class, and a boy less than five feet tall at the other. Some eighth-grade girls almost look like full-grown women. The least-developed boy may look as though he belongs in the fifth grade.

The passion to be like friends and classmates which absorbs teen-agers partly accounts for the acute self-consciousness that afflicts both those who have developed too rapidly and those who have not yet developed at all. The penchant for applying nicknames to classmates who are different means that the well-developed girl or boy is likely to be called "Rosie the Elephant," "Two Ton Tony," or the "Mountain that Walks like a Man." The under-developed boy may be called "Pipsqueak," "Runt," "Weed." A group of mothers of eighth-graders discussed their children's fears of being oversized, undersized or different in other ways. The mothers concluded that almost every child at this stage has some serious concern. He thinks he is either too big or too small, or is not as well-developed in some particular (voice, hair on face or chest, height, weight, body build) as most of his classmates.

Such concerns therefore would seem to be normal. However, many of today's parents could testify that some concerns and fears they felt in their adolescent days have had a lasting effect. To this day, one truly beautiful woman thinks people are sarcastic when they refer to her as attractive. She developed early and at thirteen was at least a head taller than everyone else in her class. She was ridiculed so often by classmates that she is still self-conscious about her appearance. Some men who seem beset by a compulsion to try to engage in intercourse with every woman they meet, can trace their obsession to embarrassment because of a real or imagined lack of masculine qualities as teen-agers. Now they spend their time proving to themselves that they have the power to charm women and are no longer objects of scorn.

This is not to say that every child with fears about his appearance will grow up with a stunted outlook. Almost everyone has some adolescent worries but grows out of them to lead a reasonably normal life. But in this area you can help your child to a more realistic and a happier outlook.

Explain to him that growth rates are different, that the undersized boy of twelve may well be the six-footer of eighteen, that you would seek medical attention if his development were out of the ordinary in any way. By doing this you can give him the reassurance he needs that he is not lacking in the essential characteristics of his sex.

Since children of different racial backgrounds tend to develop at different rates, it is likely that your child's development will follow your own, at least in a general way. Your own experience, either as one who reached maturity earlier or later than the average, may convince your youngster that he too will get there eventually. Even if he were ultimately to be taller or shorter than average, you could point to examples on the street, in shops, or from everyday experiences to show that girls taller than six feet or boys shorter than five feet lead normal lives as wives and mothers or husbands and fathers.

HOW A MOTHER SHOULD PREPARE
HER DAUGHTER FOR PUBERTY

When their daughters are eleven or twelve, many mothers think it is time to prepare them for menstruation. The subject may be introduced in an offhand way: Mother may be with her daughter when she buys sanitary napkins at the drugstore and casually mentions what they are for. Even if she has explained their purpose before, her daughter may not have a clear idea of what they are used for. The subject might also be brought up casually if one of the daughter's friends is developing physically at a faster rate. The mother might comment that soon the friend probably will begin to menstruate as well. In this way, she not only prepares her daughter for menstruation, but also instills the idea that this is experienced by all women, and is not something to be expected with dread. How menstruation might be explained is outlined in Part Two.

At eleven or twelve, some girls are fairly well-developed and have begun to menstruate. Some may not menstruate until their thirteenth or fourteenth year. Those who have not done so though their friends have begun may fear that they will lack some of the physical equipment of womanhood. This worry may be greater in areas where girls date at early ages. Girls who menstruate at fourteen or fifteen will be less likely to be concerned about their late development if no dating patterns make them feel inferior.

Some doctors think that concern among teen-age girls over the size of the bosom is more pronounced than it has ever been, the bosom having become a symbol in our society of a girl's sex appeal. Occasionally, mothers encourage this false set of values by asking a doctor to speed up nature's growth or by outfitting their daughters in garments which give the illusion of development.

Such overemphasis of the bosom can have a permanent effect upon a child's attitudes. The faculty given to women by God whereby they can give to their children not only food but warmth and affection is now regarded in the American culture as nothing more valuable than a symbol of sexiness. This is absurd. Good sense and her own mother should tell her that what makes her attractive is her natural womanliness, not her mammary glands.

Girls from twelve to fifteen show a more marked interest in the romantic aspect of sex than do boys of the same ages. Some may develop crushes—often on older boys or men, perhaps teachers, or friends of their fathers, or fathers of classmates, or movie stars. Generally they are more interested in boys than boys are in them. When they are in a group and a boy approaches, they may exchange whispers, furtive glances in his direction, and giggles. Some may make a remark to him and then they may go off on another round of giggles.

HOW A FATHER SHOULD PREPARE HIS SON

A father should tell his son of twelve to expect soon to experience significant body changes. The majority of boys do not do so until a year or more later, however. As with girls, the first important sign of adolescence is a much more rapid rate of growth. Then the testicles increase in size, producing a male hormone which, among other things, causes the voice to become lower and more resonant. Now the penis also begins to grow. It continues to enlarge until the age of eighteen or so.

Sometimes a boy becomes greatly concerned if he is not as tall as his classmates or if he observes in bathhouses or locker rooms that other boys seem more sexually developed than he. He may need reassurance that he too will have all of the physical equipment for manhood, and that the size of the sexual organs or the presence of hair on the face or chest, under the arms or in the pubic area has nothing to do with virility.

While boys at this age are still mostly interested in the company of other boys, they too are developing a greater interest in sex. Sometimes they decide that there are two aspects to it—one confined to friends, which may involve using dirty words and telling dirty jokes, and another aspect which is restrained and circumspect. A few of their friends may use vulgar sexual expressions more or less habitually. Others in their group may know that the words have a sexual connotation and a forbidden quality, but they may not really understand what the words mean.

As boys develop sexually, their previous hostile attitudes towards girls become tempered quite a bit. They may keenly enjoy just talking to girls or trading wisecracks with them. However, they generally continue to prefer the company of boys as a regular thing and will continue to do so for several years more unless adults or prevailing customs in the community exert some kind of pressure upon them to date girls.

As the testicles increase their production of hormones, there will be an increasing physical urge to release semen from the penis. At the age of fourteen many boys experience their first nocturnal emission—the discharge of semen during sleep. This discharge may or may not be accompanied by dreams of a sexual content. When this happens, a boy may be alarmed unless he has been prepared in advance by his father. He should know, of course, that this is a perfectly normal occurrence, and that even if he had sexual dreams in connection with it, no element of guilt is involved.

During the mid-teens (fifteen and sixteen) there is a quickening of interest in the physical details of the sexual act. Girls will be curious about the nature of the father's participation, the wife's reactions to her husband's advances, a mother's feelings while carrying a baby, a mother's thoughts and experiences while giving birth.

Girls may be more willing to discuss the sexual act with their girl friends, and there may be a secret handing back and forth of material which describes how intercourse takes place. A girl who has been encouraged to discuss such matters with her mother may ask less about the marital act than about pregnancy.

At this time, many strong attitudes about childbearing may be created. If a mother describes pregnancy either as something to be avoided or something to be put up with only as a last resort, the girl will come to feel that it is better to do without children. On the other hand, if the mother describes pregnancy as it is for most women—a time of relative physical discomfort, but well worthwhile because its end result is a new life brought into the world —her daughter will not have an unrealistic dread of pregnancy. Some mothers, themselves badly trained, feel compelled to describe to their daughters in complete detail the horrors of the delivery room, recounting every agonizing pain. Such tales instill a fear of conception and childbirth and encourage the daughter to avoid conception if possible.

TEEN-AGERS WHO "KNOW IT ALL"

At the age of fifteen or so, boys and girls may discuss

various methods of avoiding conception that they have heard about. They may also show an awareness of the fact that some unmarried people, as well as the married, engage in coitus. Perhaps in an indirect way, they may let slip that friends or acquaintances already have had intercourse. In any event, they often pick up various bits of information from friends, reading material, movies or television shows, and may make flat statements which give the impression that they have much more knowledge than they really do.

Probably every parent of teen-agers at some time has been taken aback by such know-it-all displays. Boys and girls often make such statements for several reasons. If they feel perverse, they may do it to observe their parents' reactions. They may be determined to prove that in this, as in other matters, they have minds of their own. They may want to show that their sources of information are superior to those their parents possess. They may display their "superiority" not only as regards sex knowledge, but also regarding food, clothing, politics and religion. Their attitude can be annoying, but this phase passes if the parents do not react to it too strongly.

A girl of sixteen who has dated only occasionally may feel that the world has passed her by and that she is destined to become an old maid. She may need frequent reassurances that most persons of her age are still engaged primarily in the work of completing their education and are not ready for serious romantic involvement.

The age of sixteen or seventeen usually marks the beginning of regular dating for the average boy and girl. At this age, they also tend to settle down emotionally. Parents often find that their children now have more sense and are easier to deal with. It is commonly urged upon parents of the troublesome high-school sophomore that they hold out and pray for patience, because after that the road is smoother.

At sixteen, many of the adolescent's concerns about developing as a man or woman have abated. The person of this age often is physically ready for parenthood. Additional years of schooling are required before boys and girls in our society are emotionally, intellectually or spiritually prepared to care for a family. It is during this stage of development, when the physical powers have developed but the emotional and intellectual and spiritual ones have not, that the greatest hazards of sexual intercourse exist.

At this time your child may express doubts about the moral values you have given him. He may argue that he has a right to neck and pet, and he may try to dismiss his parents as old-fashioned and out of touch with reality when they put a brake on his activities. However, he may not really believe what he says. He merely expresses these ideas for the sake of arguing the question. If your child has been exposed to idealistic teaching and examples for seventeen or eighteen years, probably no one would be more shocked than he if you were to tell him that he has convinced you that he is right, and that no limits should be placed upon his passion.

YOU KNOW MORE THAN YOUR TEEN-AGER!

In order to fulfill your obligation as a parent during this critical period when your child may be developing perma-. nent habits of thought and action, you might remember this fundamental principle: *By your own training and experience, you know more than your children.* You have the right to give your child proper guidance during this period. You not only have the right; you have the duty to see that he has good understanding of Christian values and walks along the path of good conduct.

It is strange that many parents must be reminded that they know more about this subject than their children. Today's world places such an overemphasis upon the prerogatives of the young that adolescents often are thought to know more about life, and to have a greater ability to handle temptations, than they actually do. For various reasons, many parents seem to have been taken in by the propaganda that their own knowledge and experience no longer are valid. But you have the priceless experience of your own adolescence and of knowing how your own sex education might have been strengthened. If you recall your own teen years, you may better understand the temptations that young people face and the safeguards that their parents must often set up to help them avoid or resist them.

Recently a middle-aged man discovered that his eighteen-year-old son was seeing a great deal of a widow in her early thirties. The son insisted that his relationship with the woman was strictly platonic. The father might have accepted this explanation except that he recalled a similar experience in his own youth when he, too, had been befriended by an older woman. His own parents had strictly forbidden him to see the woman again. At the time, he thought they were bigoted and intolerant, and insensitive to the finer aspects of human friendship. Soon thereafter, the woman took up with a classmate of his, and within six months the young man was pressured to marry her in order to give their child a name. In the light of his personal experience, and the knowledge that such friendships are at best imprudent, and can be highly dangerous, the father likewise forbade his son from seeing the older woman.

Of course, the son protested violently, insisting that his

father was entirely wrong, and sulked for weeks. At this point some parents would have relented, perhaps thinking that the most important thing was to retain the youngster's friendship. They would be mistaken. As one father commented to a friend after laying down the law to one of his children, "I did not become a parent to enter a popularity contest. Sure, I want my children to like me. But more than that, I want them to respect me. Above all, after they have grown up and can look back on their childhood, I want them to be able to realize that their parents did the right thing for them even though they did not like it at the time."

All of us can remember things we wanted in our childhood and adolescence which later experience tells us would not have been good for us. Most of us are grateful to our own parents for denying things we wanted but which we did not have enough knowledge to realize would be harmful. The parent who will win his children's lasting affection and respect gives them what they need—not necessarily what they want.

GIVE YOUR CHILD A STANDARD TO ACT BY

If, as I have suggested previously, you have impressed your children with the importance of always doing what God wants them to do, they will have a standard that will be especially valuable at this time. When it becomes necessary to direct your children along certain lines, it will not be you alone who is talking. You will be able to point to a standard that is bigger than both of you.

By this, I do not mean that the law of God should be invoked every time you have a problem with your children. The parent finding that children respond to teaching based upon the Commandments may be tempted to use this means of winning obedience even in relatively trivial matters. For example, some lyrics of popular songs are not as clean as we would like, but on the other hand, the average youngster probably pays little attention to them. The mother who forbade her teen-agers to listen to any "pop" records on this ground would be an extremist. By invoking the law of God to support her stand, she might be technically correct, but she would certainly weaken her effectiveness in the long run. As in all things, the most effective course in sex education is the moderate course.

What must be avoided is scrupulosity. This is the condition which makes a person so afraid he might offend God that the fear of sin permeates his every activity. Such a person cannot enjoy his religion. He fears to receive the Holy Eucharist because a temptation flashed through his mind after he left the Confessional. He finds his eyes drawn to a photograph of a sexy girl in a newspaper, and fears that he has committed sin. He fears contacts with the opposite sex because he finds a strange sense of desire created. In brief, he is forever fearful that even the normal, natural acts of everyday living may be sinful—or at least occasions of sin.

You need not worry about instilling scrupulosity in your children if you yourself adopt reasonable, moderate attitudes. To do so, you will probably have to refer to your own experience and observations.

As a general principle, you should keep your children from engaging in practices that are obviously wrong for almost everyone. In this category might be placed the practice of girls wearing the equivalent of two small handkerchiefs as their total covering at the beach. The girl who wears such an outfit provokes impure thoughts by the males who see her, and encourages sinful approaches. Likewise, there is no doubt that the theater or cabaret that features immodest, if not immoral, acts is a scene of impure thoughts for most boys and men. The whole purpose of such acts is to stimulate passion.

Some practices may be harmless for most people and potentially sinful for relatively few. In this category might be placed off-color jokes. The reading of certain magazines also belongs in this category, although there are publications which specialize in hard-core pornography. A motion picture that does not belabor suggestive scenes, although accentuating the female form, would not be a source of serious temptation to the average youngster. Nor would the usual television program.

Many practices fall into a gray area. Depending upon specific circumstances, they may or may not be proximate occasions of sin. For instance, there is nothing morally wrong with a young man driving a girl about in an automobile, nor would anything be wrong if he parked the car in order to chat with her. On the other hand, a proximate occasion of sin probably would exist if he parked in a secluded spot, knowing that he and his companion would likely neck there undisturbed for a long period of time.

Of course, no parent can or should stand guard over her children every minute to keep them from being exposed to moral hazards, any more than the mother of a schoolboy should take him to school every day to keep him from being run over. A youngster must gradually learn to accept responsibility for his own moral welfare. The older he gets, the more responsibility he will have to take.

You will find that the major question in dealing with your teen-ager (not only in matters of sex but in all other areas of his life as well) will be how much direction you should give and how much freedom you should allow. Most conflicts between teen-agers and parents revolve around this very question. Youngsters want more of the *privileges* of adults than their parents think they should have—and the parents try to impose more of the *duties* of adulthood than the youngsters are willing to accept.

Here again, your understanding of the nature of the adolescent, based upon your own experience, will prove immensely helpful. Most youngsters will put up what they consider a fight for freedom, but they are usually secretly or unconsciously unhappy when they get more freedom than they can really handle. Most youngsters want controls. In moments of candid conversation they may acknowledge this fact and express their appreciation to their parents for laying down the law on occasion. It is a paradoxical fact that the most respected teachers in a high school are very often the strictest. Those who let the youngsters "get away with murder" are lightly regarded and sometimes do not even have their pupils' respect.

Don't allow yourself to be fooled by loose talk about "democracy." Democracy in political life is fine but it has less place in a parent's dealings with minor children. Just as God is not a "democrat" but has set down His laws because He knows what is best for us, so should parents set down the rules which tell their children what is allowable and what is not. Your goal, however, should be to allow your growing child to make more and more of his own decisions. By giving him more and more self-rule, you are more likely to have a child who can stand on his own feet as a responsible adult when he is twenty-one.

Maintaining control over your youngsters, while gradually giving them more and more freedom to act for themselves, is a task that requires a great deal of common sense and patience. In trying their wings, they will doubtless make mistakes. But they will learn something in the process. If you try to save them from minor mistakes, you will be denying them the chance to grow. On the other hand, you should make sure that their mistakes will not be truly serious—the kind which could cause severe heartaches or ruin their lives.

If you can maintain open lines of communication with your teen-agers, so that you are able to discuss matters frankly with them, you will find that this process of gradually allowing them more and more freedom will develop more smoothly than would otherwise be the case. If your children start with the basic idea that you are not trying to act as a policeman and are interested solely in their welfare, a solid basis will be established. For various reasons, not all youngsters are frank with their parents. If this is so in your family, it would be helpful if they had an older person of their own sex in whom they could confide freely, discussing their temptations and the hazards they face. Fortunate are those girls who can tell their problems to a nun or other adult, and those boys who can speak frankly to a priest, religious brother, older relative or friend.

The art of rulership is involved here. If you have good relations with your children, they will be more likely to accept the ideas you stand for. They will not feel oppressed in doing so.

Recently a girl of seventeen, a high-school senior, asked her mother if she could attend an all-night graduation party at a neighboring beach which some classmates had organized. Discussing the matter calmly, the mother learned that no chaperones were planned and that some boys would have the use of the family car overnight. Some of the lads also were known as heavy drinkers, and alcohol seemed likely to be greatly in evidence at the party. The mother explained to her daughter that such parties had caused personal tragedies and public scandal in the past. The girl protested that her mother had a suspicious mind and that such parties were common. The mother firmly held her ground over the daughter's protests. Naturally, the girl was hostile toward her parents before the party.

The day after the event, however, the girl's mood changed abruptly. The affair had got completely out of hand; police had brought several boys to the station house for disturbing the peace; several couples had been caught on the beach in compromising positions. "I'm glad you didn't let me go," she told her mother.

SOCIETY AND TEEN-AGE IMMORALITY

Why must you do the job of looking after your child's chastity—and not count on society to help you? In a nationally syndicated series of articles on teen-age immorality, writers Martin and Marcia Abramson listed these statistics:

Juvenile arrests have increased 116 per cent in the United States in the last ten years. The cost of youth crime has increased to four billion dollars a year. The number of young people under eighteen years who were jailed has increased to a million a year. The number of young people between the ages of ten and seventeen with court records for misbehavior has increased greatly.

The number of illegitimate births reported to the U.S. Public Health Service has increased to a quarter of a million a year—an increase of 60 per cent over the past ten years and an increase of 300 per cent over the last twenty-five years. More than 1500 pregnant girls under the age of sixteen were dropped from New York City schools in 1962. Chicago's schools lost 576 pregnant students, including one who became pregnant at the age of eleven. Washington, D.C., schools lost 265 between the ages of twelve and fifteen. In Washington, one out of every five babies is born out of wedlock.

"We have traditionally classed the unwed mother as a

shiftless dolt who comes out of a slum," the Abramsons wrote. "But in the maternity homes for unwed mothers run by the Volunteers of America, most of the girls show a surprising degree of intelligence and a good educational background. Few come from families on public assistance.

"Indeed, the greatest percentage of increase in the ranks of those who breed illegitimate progeny are products of so-called good families on the right side of the tracks. All too often, the promiscuous teen-aged mother comes from middle-and-high-income suburbia, so the true facts of their maternity may be conveniently doctored in the public records."

That there is a vast five-million-dollar-a-year business in pornography—directed mainly at teen-agers, and even distributed at playgrounds and schoolyards—is affirmed by no less an authority than J. Edgar Hoover, director of the Federal Bureau of Investigation. In an article in *This Week* magazine, Mr. Hoover stated:

> Distribution of pornographic material prepared especially for juveniles is now so efficient that it is quite accurate to say that no child is beyond its reach. The fact that millions of innocent children are exposed in their formative years to reading matter and art depicting shocking sexual travesties is reason enough for serious dismay. Much more important, however, is the growing conviction among law officers that the flood of pornography that has been circulating among our young people for the past ten years is a major factor in today's rapidly rising rate of sex crime.
>
> Last Fall our agents arrested a veteran dealer who had just replenished his stock of obscene items. His car was found to contain 18,000 items of pornography in the form of "comic" books, decks of cards, photographs and tiny, palm-sized booklets of lewd jokes

and anecdotes, many destined for distribution at schools. The man himself valued the haul at $20,000! As we well know, such items do not reach only one youngster but quickly spread through a school being sold, loaned and re-sold until they are either confiscated or worn out.

Even more distressing is evidence brought to light by Senate investigations that large numbers of our young people are being lured into acting as "pushers," and even manufacturers of this material. In a respectable country-like community near New York City a group of teen-agers was recently arrested for such activities. They included a girl and boy who posed for crudely erotic photographs, an eighteen-year-old friend who took the pictures and three other youths, of whom the eldest was 17.

To understand the prevailing moral climate to which young people are now exposed, we must realize that many people are in favor of a new code of sexual morality. For example, Dr. Alan Guttmacher, president of the Planned Parenthood Federation, has expressed himself in favor of giving instructions to high-school students on how to make use of contraceptives. And Dr. Peter Henderson, principal medical officer of Britain's Ministry of Education, has stated publicly that premarital sexual relations are not immoral "if a young man and woman are in love and intend to get married."

It is a mistake to think that immorality is not to be found in "nice" upper-class neighborhoods. The sad fact is that it is perhaps equally prevalent among people who are comfortable and well-off than among the poor.

For example, in the prosperous suburb of Darien, Connecticut, where can be found the homes of many of New

York's most successful business and professional men, a report by a committee of parents found that teen-age behavior had reached a point of alarm. This survey indicated that there was an "unbelievable amount" of necking and petting among junior-high-school pupils at a local theater, and "an alarming number of pregnancies in high school." One Darien girl told the group that "accepting a date to a drive-in movie is like accepting a date for sexual relations."

It is no exaggeration to say that a similar report, making identically the same findings, could be made in hundreds if not thousands of other communities.

If you wish to keep your child uncontaminated by the conditions described above, you should realize that he will face countless temptations to do evil—and only your constant watchfulness and guidance will keep him out of harm's reach.

THE GREATEST MORAL HAZARD FOR BOYS

The most pressing problem for the teen-age boy, and sometimes until he marries and even afterwards, is that of masturbation. This is a widespread practice.

All deliberate masturbation is wrong for the reason that the intentional encouragement of sexual pleasure outside the act of intercourse by married people is a sin. In terms of a boy's development, and his moral stature over a long period, the chronic masturbator is a serious problem to himself. And while less common, masturbation by girls is increasing, according to many authorities, perhaps as a result of the modern teaching that girls too have the right to enjoy sex as often as they wish.

It is probably true that most masturbators do not consciously and deliberately set out to engage in self-abuse.

Rather, their action results from tensions they have allowed or perhaps encouraged, and succumbing to sin reflects an unwillingness or inability to end these tensions in any other way.

It is important to realize what masturbation is and what it is not. Although the word is used to describe the touching and rubbing of the genitals by very young children, this obviously is not sinful. As we discussed in the chapter dealing with the young child, his curiosity about his sex organs is no different from his curiosity about his nose, ears or mouth. Just as no guilt is involved when the young baby puts his toes in his mouth, there is no guilt associated with his feeling his genitals and experiencing the sense of touch.

It is not masturbation when the boy has an erection of his penis. Dwelling upon sexual thoughts may result in an erection, but it is also caused by a large variety of innocent factors, for example, stimulation from tight clothing, pressure exerted by the bladder, and some glandular disturbances. Quite often, normal boys will awaken with an erection. Obviously, therefore, having an erection in itself is no sin.

Nor is it masturbation when the genitals are rubbed when no sexual pleasure is intended. Sometimes the penis or vulva may itch and a boy or girl may scratch it to relieve the itch. In washing it is often necessary and desirable to cleanse the sex organs thoroughly. Obviously, there is nothing wrong with touching or rubbing these organs for such purposes.

Sinful masturbation, with which we are concerned here, is the deliberate manipulation of the penis (of the boy) or vulva (of the girl) in order to produce sexual satisfaction. If this manipulation is carried to its natural conclusion, which would be an orgasm, it is mortally sinful.

As a parent, what can you do to correct this practice or at least to keep it from growing into an insidious habit which might persist until your child's marriage or even longer? It is first necessary to understand exactly what factors cause masturbation.

USUAL CAUSES OF MASTURBATION

Perhaps the foremost cause is the physical urge itself. At the time of adolescence, when the sexual organs are developing, the glands are secreting hormones and setting up strange unfamiliar feelings. The adolescent boy or girl experiences desires which were previously unknown. Ordinary contacts with the opposite sex, the sight of the opposite sex in photographs, romantic daydreams, all may produce a feeling of pleasurable anticipation which the young person has not felt before and is not prepared to cope with.

Even if a boy were isolated from everything which might produce thoughts of sex, his very nature, calling for the occasional discharge of semen from his body at night, would introduce him to the feeling of pleasure which such a discharge produces. These nocturnal emissions, or "wet dreams," are often accompanied by fantasies in which the boy imagines himself in sexual situations. Of course, it is perfectly natural and innocent when the boy has an orgasm in such dreams and does nothing consciously to encourage it.

A second cause of masturbation may be simple curiosity. Teen-agers tend to boast about their new-found powers of masculinity or femininity and some may think they should make sure that they are also developing to the full.

Sometimes boys are drawn into this habit by others— usually older boys—who encourage them to engage in the sin and show them how to do it. One boy may excite the other's imagination by recounting all the pleasure which the act involves, and beat down the younger one's fear of sin and sense of modesty with the argument that "everybody does it."

A third cause may be accidental. Unplanned physical contacts may give pleasant sensations. The teen-ager may then make future sensations deliberate, developing a sense of eagerness which feeds upon itself until an orgasm is achieved.

Once the youngster has experienced relief from sexual tension, he may turn to it whenever he feels worried, insecure, unwanted or rejected. The act of masturbation then becomes a means by which he compensates himself for real or imagined wrongs committed against him. Masturbation of this chronic type has been likened to habitual recourse to alcohol, when a person turns to drink to soothe a battered ego.

Once the crutch of masturbation is found, the individual is tempted to use it more and more often. This is particularly true with youngsters who are shy or timid by nature. According to psychotherapists, such boys experience greater feelings of guilt after sinning in this way than do extroverted, out-going types. The sense of shame and weakness of will that the masturbator feels then tends to increase his feelings of inadequacy, frustration or loneliness. In moments of stress, he then becomes even more likely to turn to this infantile behavior.

Not long ago, it was generally believed that repeated masturbation could cause a wide variety of physical and mental ailments—skin diseases, deafness, tuberculosis, impotency, even insanity. Scientists have found no bases in fact for such beliefs. Psychotherapists tell us, however, that the youngster who fails again and again to control his impulses may develop deep feelings of guilt and inferiority.

He may draw within himself, may show no interest in family or friends, and may exhibit neurotic patterns which may persist for a long time.

Masturbation is a sin and can neither be condoned nor tolerated. However, this is perhaps the foremost example of a situation in which, while we hate the sin, we also must love the sinner. Almost every authority who is familiar with the adolescent mind agrees that the worst possible way to handle this practice is to punish the youngster suspected of it or even caught at it. The unfortunate truth is that the more parents or teachers call attention to this practice, the more securely it seems to become entrenched.

How, then, can you help your child avoid the habit? Since chronic masturbation almost always results from loneliness, frustration, and feelings that he is inferior or is not appreciated, the best thing to do is reassure him often of his intrinsic worth as an individual and of your unquestioned love for him.

There will be times when moods of depression will come upon him. The causes of such moods may seem trivial, even absurd. He has not been invited to a party. He has failed to make the first team. The teacher has made an unkind remark to him. A friend has reported what someone has said about him behind his back. He did his geometry homework faithfully, yet received a failing mark.

On such occasions, it will be your task to assure your youngster, in a gentle and affectionate way, that such moods are characteristic of teen-agers generally. Perhaps you can recall, for his benefit, instances in your own life when it seemed that your whole world was about to crumble. You might point out that time heals all wounds—that those incidents that caused you such pain seem much less significant today than they appeared at the moment.

If you realize that your youngster's fits of depression,

moodiness and antagonism are but passing phases, you will be better able to cope with them. Even the best of teen-agers are often extremely difficult to live with. They say and do things that cause their parents to despair. You must have faith that time is on your side—that the problems of adolescence will pass away after a few years. If you can develop this outlook, you may be better able to display the patience which is so important for you to have at this stage of your child's development.

It is also advisable to encourage him in activities which will use up some of his abundant energy and at the same time take his mind off himself and his problems. Sports are an ideal outlet—preferably those he can engage in, but also those which he can watch with an enthusiastic interest. Encourage him to take part in other school ac-tivities—the school band, photography club, school news-paper.

Try especially to find some outlet for any special talents he may have. The youngster who is the best ping-pong player in his class, or gets the best marks in math, or is up-to-date on the latest dance steps, or is the acknowledged expert on major league baseball batting averages, or has other distinctive talents, will have a greater self-esteem to defend himself against feelings of depression which may come upon him.

You can also exercise control over many of the influ-ences which might create erotic thoughts in your child's mind. Some movies, television programs, books and maga-zines are deliberately designed to stir up thoughts of sex. Teen-age boys are highly susceptible to these things. With-out being an extremist or fanatic, try to keep out such influences.

While some youngsters will spend a great deal of time by themselves at this age, you should discourage this prac-tice from becoming excessive. It is particularly unwise to allow your youngster to spend much time awake in bed. His thoughts may turn to sex from sheer boredom as much as from anything else. For this reason, set a pattern early in the child's life of encouraging him to get out of bed as soon as he is awake. You might teach him to prepare his own breakfast, so that he can start his day even though you are asleep.

TRAINING FOR CHASTITY

When we say that the adolescent has a natural instinct to relieve his sexual tensions and that many of the most powerful influences in our society encourage this release, we are merely explaining pressures which might lead to masturbation. To cite reasons why a boy might masturbate is a far cry, however, from giving him an excuse for doing it. Although it may sometimes be difficult to resist those pressures from within himself and those imposed by the influences of society, he nevertheless has a moral obligation to do so.

Is this an unreasonable position? Of course not—especially when we consider that the whole story of man is his ability to dominate himself and to train his instincts. It is precisely this ability that makes man what he is—an intelligent creature with control over his own destiny. If he lacked the ability to discipline himself, he would be a mere animal—and we could condone any and all sexual acts just as we condone any such acts performed by animals.

True, the urge toward sexual relief is a physical urge, and in that sense is natural. But when we say that it must be harnessed for the good of the whole man, we do not set up a rule which applies only in this one particular case. Examples of this need to harness our instincts exist all about us.

If someone steps on your feet in a crowded bus, you

might be instinctively tempted to push him off—even to punch him in retaliation. But your training would triumph over your instincts. You probably would ask him politely to get off your feet or—at most—tell him to get off with irritation in your voice. If you were on the same crowded bus and felt the pangs of hunger, you would not take a sandwich from your lunch pail and begin to munch on it —although your hunger would be instinctual. No, you would wait for a more suitable time, even though it meant enduring hunger pains a while longer.

Or consider man's natural instincts to avoid work and do things the easy way. If he has several miles to travel, he would usually rather ride than walk. But this would hardly justify his climbing into any automobile he saw and driving it off.

You could cite numerous other examples to your child to show that when God tells us not to use our sexual powers except under specified conditions, He is not demanding anything exceptional. You might cite the lowly bread knife with the sharp cutting edges. Everyone accepts the fact that you can use this knife to cut foods but must not use it to cut people. Or take the automobile: it can be driven only in certain ways and by qualified people. In many states, no one under the age of eighteen may drive a car and at no time can one drive on the wrong side of the road or faster than the law allows.

When examples like these are used, most adolescents have no difficulty in accepting the fact that God has given them sexual powers to be used only in the way He intended. This means that they must not indulge in sexual pleasure until they are married.

To make this point is not enough, however. Your teenager must realize that he will have to exercise this control over his sexual powers all his life. If he believes that chastity is only for the unmarried, he will be poorly prepared for marriage. He will be like many young people who think that "the lid is off" and "anything goes" the moment the ring is placed upon the finger.

The truth is that a happy and harmonious married life is impossible without chastity. Many people have a wrong idea about what chastity means. Because priests, nuns and brothers take a vow of chastity, some people think chastity means that a person must never know a sexual relationship. This is untrue. Chastity is nothing more or less than using our sexual organs in the way God intended. For the priest, nun and brother, that means abstaining from sex, because they are unmarried. All other unmarried people (those who have never married and widows, widowers or those separated from their lawfully-wedded husbands or wives) also must abstain. For married people, chastity means that they may indulge in sexual intimacy only with each other—and at times and in a way which conform to the laws God has given us.

Everybody must be chaste, therefore. Married men or women have no right to engage in sex whenever or wherever the mood strikes. They must obey certain rules governing their own relationships. For example, a man is away from his wife on a trip for several weeks. He feels a desire for sexual release, but his obligation to be faithful means that he cannot indulge it.

Or suppose his wife is ill for a long period of time and is unable to engage in the marital act. He must abstain just as an unmarried person must. Most doctors urge couples to abstain from intercourse for five or six weeks before a child is born, and for three or four weeks afterwards. This period of abstinence thus may run two months or longer. A husband who succumbed to his physical impulses and had intercourse with someone other than his wife during that period would be guilty of sin, of course.

The point is that you should let your child know that

the mastery over self which he achieves in his teens will make life better for him as an adult. He could be said to be "going to school" during his period of adolescence, for what he learns about resisting temptation at the age of fourteen will serve him in good stead at the age of forty.

THE POSITIVE VALUE OF CHASTITY

It will be difficult if not impossible to instill the habit of chastity in your youngster unless you can give him a clear picture of why it is so important. We often meet young people who have been told all about sex and who may know even better than their parents the whole anatomical story of what happens in coitus. They also have been told that in our society it is not "nice" for unmarried people to have intercourse. But without having a real reason to abstain until marriage, they are tempted to eat the forbidden fruit because some of their friends say it is grand.

To withstand the influences of the times and the urges of their own bodies, your youngsters need a deep and vital appreciation of the awe-inspiring gift which God has given them. This power to bring a human life into existence—a living, breathing, thinking infant capable of gaining eternal life with God in heaven—is truly a marvelous thing. It is in fact a sacred power, and the body which possesses this power should also remain sacred.

A person to whose care a precious stone was entrusted would guard it with his life, keeping it under lock and key and taking every precaution to prevent it from being lost or stolen. This power to procreate a human life is certainly more precious than any gem man has ever seen—and it should be guarded with even greater care.

You will have more success in instilling chastity if you stress its positive values, rather than harp on the evil effects which come from the failure to practice it. The way we human beings are made, it is usually easier to get us to move toward something good we want, rather than to keep away from something we do not want. This characteristic seems even more marked among teen-agers.

A mother wanted her children to take vitamin supplements. Each evening at dinner, she passed pills around to each of her four boys. Night after night they protested. Endlessly, she told them that they needed the vitamins to prevent colds and to ward off many other ailments. Despite her repeated lectures, their objections persisted.

When the oldest boy went to high school, he joined the freshman basketball team. In the course of training, the coach emphasized to the boys the importance of a diet that included milk, fruit, vegetables. He added that it wouldn't be a bad idea to take a vitamin pill every day.

The boy's attitude changed immediately. Because he looked up to the coach, instead of resisting the vitamin pill at dinner, he now began to ask for it. His younger brothers followed his example.

If by your teaching and example your child *wills* to be chaste, he will find that more than half his battle is won. There is no disputing the strong physical urges which normal youngsters feel, but on the other hand this urge is not so uncontrollable as many moderns think. Left to himself, and without constant reminders from outside, the sexual urge can remain dormant for remarkably long periods of time.

Nevertheless, tempting thoughts do crowd in and suggestions of sex are introduced from the outside. A young person will inevitably face many situations during which he will have to struggle to rid these thoughts from his mind. If he is wise, he will seek to change the subject as forcefully as he can.

The need to keep a teen-ager's mind occupied can hardly be overstressed. The youngster who is on the go all the time—either at school, at his homework, engaging in sports or other physical activities during his free time—will have that much less time in which to be tempted. Moreover, the physical activities he engages in will use up much of his energy and leave him with little left to be expended in the pursuit of sexual pleasure.

If you can devise ways of keeping your youngsters engrossed in things outside themselves, you will go a long way toward providing outlets for their energy and diversions for their minds. One family with five boys has a basketball net set up in the yard, shuffleboard, ping-pong and a generous supply of games and phonograph records in the basement. There is something doing in this home almost every minute, and it is likely that the amount of time devoted to the harboring of sexual thoughts is kept to a minimum.

Naturally, you cannot climb into your child's mind. However, if he seems moody, you might try to snap him out of it by suggesting activities that require all of his concentration and help keep his mind on worthwhile objectives. Even a game of cards in the evening, a trip downtown to do some shopping, watching a favorite television program, taking a walk, practicing dance steps, playing miniature golf in the yard—all these diversions will help keep his mind constructively occupied and afford him little opportunity for sexual fantasies.

If you can encourage him to change the subject mentally whenever dangerous thoughts intrude, you will teach him an extremely valuable lesson for life. For it is a fact that habits of dealing with one's thoughts often are developed in adolescence and stay with one all the rest of his years. The young man who learns early how to turn off temptations will learn a technique for self-discipline which will help him in many other ways as well.

The greatest defense against this sin is spiritual, of course. If you have instructed him properly, he will know that if he uses his organs in a wrong way he offends the Creator. He will naturally wish to avoid sins of impurity.

Due to man's fall from grace as a result of the sin of our first parents, however, the urge to masturbate in young people is often quite strong. It may even be stronger than the typical well-taught youngster is able to cope with. When and if he falls from grace, he should realize that the Sacraments of Penance and the Holy Eucharist will cleanse his soul, just as soap and water will cleanse his body.

Generally you can use somewhat more pressure in getting him to the Confessional than to the Holy Eucharist. The reason is that a youngster in a state of sin almost invariably has a sense of shame and guilt, and often will welcome the opportunity to confess and make a firm resolution to avoid the sins in the future. It is difficult to make a bad Confession, because the youngster usually is anxious to restore himself to the state of grace.

On the other hand, too much pressure to receive the Holy Eucharist may have an adverse effect. We all know, of course, that one can receive the Eucharist unworthily and this possibility is increased if a person is virtually forced to the altar rail against his will.

Not all of a youngster's reluctance to receive the Eucharist may be traced to the fact that he is in a state of sin. Teen-agers sometimes go through a crisis in faith. Coming into contact with persons holding different religious beliefs, and with those who hold no beliefs at all, a young person may seriously question some teachings of his faith that he has taken for granted until now. He may observe that other people lead good lives without ever partaking of the Eucharist. Friends may tell him that going to Communion is for sissies and—if the men in his family seldom go to the altar—he may think that it is more masculine to do what the older men do.

The problem is to encourage him to go, without making it seem that you are forcing him. One mother makes it a point to go to Confession after dinner on the first Saturday each month. She announces her plans at dinner and offers to take any of her four children who wish to go with her. Those who do not wish to go are not required to give reasons for refusing. A child who lets more than a month go by without Holy Communion should have a private chat with Dad along the way.

CLOTHES MAKE THE TEEN-AGER

The old axiom has it that "Appearances are often deceiving." To this axiom might be added a few more words: "Appearances are often deceiving—but more often they tell the truth at a glance."

If you recall your own experiences, you will probably agree with this amendment. When you meet a person for the first time and observe him in ordinary, everyday situations, you usually can make a fairly accurate appraisal of his economic status, educational background, social position. Talking with him a while longer, you will get a fairly good idea of how he stands on important moral questions. Simply by observing how he dresses, the amount of adornment on his person, and other things, you could reach other conclusions about many of his personal habits—whether he is flashy or sedate, inclined to be liberal or ultra-conservative in most ways of living. Of course, you would sometimes be wrong—but more often, you would be right.

There can be a definite relationship between manners and morals. It could not be otherwise. The wretched prostitute who prowls the streets of the city at night, seeking to sell her body to any available male, could hardly be expected to have the manners of a princess. Nor would someone who actually led a very moral life dress or act like a prostitute. As a general rule, then, manners and morals tend to go hand in hand.

This is true among adolescents as well. A priest who has spent his life teaching teen-agers says that when he walks into a classroom at the beginning of each school year in September, he can generally tell from the way the boys are dressed, from their expressions and general demeanor, which ones will be the best and most eager students and which ones will be indifferent. This relationship between studies and manners is so great that most Catholic schools have found that when pupils are permitted to attend class in dungarees, shorts, tight-fitting sweaters, or other garments they toss on at the last minute, they not only look like tramps but they also begin to act like them.

So it is with sex. I doubt whether any youngster has ever got into serious trouble without giving some tip-off by his manners well in advance of it. Take the example of one girl who became pregnant at the age of seventeen. Two long years before that, she began wearing tight-fitting sweaters which showed off her figure to the fullest possible extent. Then she began applying rouge, lipstick and mascara with a heavy hand, missing no tricks to attract the attention of boys. She walked as she had seen actresses do in the movies in order to invite the wolf whistles of boys who saw her.

All of these manners preceded by a long time her first intimate relationship with a boy. If her parents had been alert, they would have realized that by her actions she was telling everyone that she was ready for premarital adventures.

Of course, this is an extreme case. I do not wish to imply that girls who wear lipstick and make-up are headed for a bad end, or that they should walk around with glum faces and dresses that hang like sacks. There is a happy medium. I do say that the girl who manifests too great a deviation from normal in her actions and begins to display what her parents know perfectly well are bad manners, is taking a step in the wrong direction morally.

By their manners, boys often give many indications of what they are thinking about sex, too. For example, a boy who treats his sister with respect shows by his attitude that he has a high regard for women in general. On the other hand, the lad who is excessively fresh to girls and is not above using profanity in their presence or telling them off-color stories, is displaying the fact that he has less than an idealistic concept about sex.

It may be necessary occasionally to call your child's attention to the need for modesty in dress. Sometimes boys and girls go beyond reasonable limits in this regard, often because they innocently follow a fad and do not realize that their dress calls the attention of the opposite sex to their sexual equipment—and, when it is the girls who are immodest, arouses strong sexual desires in boys.

A good general principle is to avoid any way of dressing that unduly excites the attention of the opposite sex. Applying this principle intelligently will depend upon circumstances. A girl wearing an ordinary bathing suit might be considered perfectly modest at the beach, but if she were to reveal that much of herself on a public street far from the beach, it would be a different story. On the other hand, the girl wearing a skimpy bikini, even on the beach, would be tendering a direct invitation to boys to look and conjure up sexual thoughts.

We have seen entirely too many immaculately dressed, perfectly mannered men and women whose sex lives are utterly shameful to say that manners and morality always go together. On the other hand, and this is particularly true of young people, there is generally a strong connection between the two.

NOW IS THE TIME TO
DISCOURAGE EARLY MARRIAGE

Some parents encourage the early marriage of their youngsters in the belief that this will put an end to the danger of sexual promiscuity and in the belief that—for girls, at least—any marriage is better than spinsterhood. Actually they are seeking to avoid one or two evils with what is often a far greater one.

A little thought will convince you, I am sure, that most teen-age brides and bridegrooms are not really prepared to undertake the responsibility of raising a family. As you know from your own experience, the mother and father who bring a young life into the world have the God-given responsibility of caring for that youngster, looking after his spiritual, physical and emotional welfare until he is old enough to care for himself. And as you well know, to have a baby dependent upon you in every way is an awesome responsibility—one which youngsters in their teens are hardly prepared to undertake.

Again, cold statistics tell a conclusive story. They reveal that of every two marriages involving a girl twenty years old or younger, one is destined to be ended in the divorce courts.

Unlike non-Catholics, who consider divorce a legitimate way of ending a marriage, Catholics believe that a marriage performed before a priest is binding for life and cannot be dissolved except on the death of one partner. Thus the right choice of a marriage partner is much more important for a Catholic than for a non-Catholic, for the Catholic does not get a second, third, fourth or fifth chance. This is all the more reason why the Catholic should wait until he is quite sure that he is prepared to undertake the responsibilities of marriage.

Why discuss the question of early marriage with youngsters who may not even have begun to date? Because there is a definite relationship between the time a person first dates and the time when the wedding bells ring.

Most young people go through similar stages in their relationship with the opposite sex. First, they are thrilled with the companionship of the boy or girl, and little more than companionship is expected. Then there may be a hand-holding stage, and kissing on occasion. But as the child associates more and more with the opposite sex, more adult privileges are sought. After five or six years of dating, most persons are anxious to fulfill the desire they feel when with someone they like a great deal. This desire to express love by the means which God ordained is natural enough, but its achievement of course is permitted only to the married. So it is also natural for young people to wish to marry. If they begin dating at twelve, they will have prepared themselves (speaking generally) through their associations with the opposite sex for marriage at eighteen. If they begin dating at fourteen, their average age of marriage might be about twenty. If they begin at sixteen, when, for example, they are juniors or seniors in high school, the ordinary development of events will lead them to want to marry when they are twenty-two or so —a time when their schooling is likely to have been completed and they are old enough to fulfill the responsibilities of parenthood. Thus it would seem sensible to discourage your youngster from too great an involvement in dating until he is at least sixteen.

Many parents are making the mistake of thinking it is cute to have their youngsters dancing at the age of ten. Some mothers even go so far as to arrange parties for these very young. Teachers in high schools report that some of these hothouse flowers are far more seriously involved than their parents seem to know. In fact, one high-school principal said he thinks it an achievement if he goes through the school year without having a pregnant pupil to contend with. After seeing the consequences of early dating and going steady, most parents now are less inclined to encourage their children in such practices.

When your children are in their pre-teens, it might be well to let them know why you do not think it wise to begin dating until the later high-school or early college years. One good reason is that a young man or woman has better prospects for a good career (and the young woman has better prospects for a successful marriage) if he and she have spent at least several years at college. Due to increased demands for well-educated workers—and the sharp drop in job openings which unskilled persons can fill—an education is more important today than ever before.

You might point out that the person who fails to finish high school has dismal chances of getting a good job, and that the high-school graduate of today is perhaps no better off in this regard than the elementary-school graduate of twenty-five years ago. Therefore, the young man or woman, and especially the man, who seriously wishes to prepare for future roles as husband and father or wife and mother must spend a longer time in school than was ever necessary before. For this reason, today's children should marry later than was customary in the past, instead of earlier. This is especially important for those unprepared or unwilling to raise a large family.

You might also point out that it is extremely difficult for

teen-age brides or bridegrooms to continue with their education. First, they usually have to earn a living—and it is difficult for a person to work full time and go to school at the same time. There is also the likelihood that parenthood will interrupt all their plans to continue their schooling. The birth of a baby would require the wife to stay at home to care for it, thus preventing her from going to school or earning an income. Her husband would have to earn more money to support his family—and might have to give up his education to do it.

Young people usually appreciate the logic of these arguments, but it is well to indoctrinate them before they actually have any desire to date. At such a time, they can see the problem as a third party might see it. Later, when they themselves become personally involved, the task of convincing them will be just so much harder. For this reason, I continue to emphasize the importance of anticipating problems which will arise as your child grows older, and to create the proper attitudes ahead of time. When the child is intimately involved in a problem, he is inclined to argue from an emotional rather than a rational point of view.

THREE WAYS YOU CAN HELP
YOUR TEEN-AGER

And so, parents, you can consider that you will do a good job with your teen-ager if you give him three things:

1. *An understanding of why he lives.* Teach him that he was created by God and redeemed by Christ, that he is only a little lower than the angels in the order of creation, that he will find his complete fulfillment in serving God in this life and the next. These are the values that make for fruitful living. The well-developed religious family pro-

duces sons and daughters who will lead purposeful lives long after their parents have passed on to eternity. During the teen-age years, the child will re-examine critically many of the religious values he accepted so beautifully in childhood, and it is the parents' job to help him develop at this time a more mature approach to his religion and to his spiritual life. Sad is the boy or girl who walks into adulthood without any clear idea of what life is all about.

2. *Appreciation of his own worth.* If he sees himself as a creature of God, he must also appreciate that he is a unique creature, called by God to lead his own life and to use his talents in his own way. Ideally, there should be no "Mama's boys" or shrinking violets. Each human being is made by God to be a free human being, and he should become mature enough to know what kind of life under God he wants to lead and how to pursue that life.

3. *Strong habits of virtue.* Freedom does not mean, as some moderns would like to make it mean, the right to do anything one pleases without regard to God's demands or the rights of other people. The child must be trained to use his powers, the sexual ones and all others, moderately and modestly, not merely for his own satisfaction but for the service of others and the greater glory of God. Almost without exception, the great people of history have been those trained in the art of self-discipline, otherworldliness, and charity.

Whereas no one would dream of suddenly becoming a mechanic or an engineer, a doctor or a lawyer, without an apprenticeship or preparation, yet every day there are numbers of young men and women who marry without having given an instant's thought to preparing themselves for the arduous work of educating their children which awaits them.

—POPE PIUS XII

When Your Child Begins To Date

FOR thousands of years in many societies, it was customary for parents to exercise rigid controls over their unmarried children's associations with the other sex. In some Asiatic countries, even today, a girl and boy conceivably may not exchange more than a hundred words with each other before they are married. Not only do parents control the courtship, but they even control the choice of a marriage partner. In European countries, the practice of chaperoning was common until recent times. An unmarried boy and girl were not permitted to date unless a trusted older person accompanied them. Even today, in Spain, a single girl may find her reputation damaged if she often stays out with a boy later than 11 P.M.

In most parts of the world, however, such strict safe-guards have been eliminated. To some extent this is a good trend. But the tendency has been to go to the other extreme: the pendulum has swung from a situation in which young people had almost nothing to say over the persons they would date or the conditions of courtship, to a situation in which they have almost everything to say. Parents today seem to stand by helplessly while their children date and go steady with absolute freedom, not to say license. Just as the system of absolute parental control was bad, so too is the present system in which there is little or no supervision.

YOU MUST TALK IF YOU WOULD RULE

Much of the trouble between parents and the children old enough to begin the dating process is that they often do not talk the same language. For example, going steady may mean one thing to the youngster and quite another to the father or mother. As one girl put it, "I went steady three times last month." Obviously, therefore, it is important that the tugging parties really listen to each other, not only to the words but to what is meant by the silences and the grunts. A boy who says "You never let me go out with girls" may not quite mean what he says and certainly is not going to be won over by a logical argument showing him that he lies. What he really means is that you are riding herd on him too closely and that he is angry about it. You may still need in this case to veto his demands, but perhaps with more persuasive reasons.

This means that a parent must be a good talker, and a judicious one. She must know when to acquiesce to a son or daughter immediately, when to call for discussion before granting permission, and when to say No. Our Lord once said, "Watch and pray lest ye enter into temptation." Many parents pray for their children but forget that Christ mentioned vigilance before prayer.

Some parents on the other hand are proficient only at yelling. They seem surprised, particularly as the adolescent grows older, that the only result is a deaf ear, except when he is yelling in return.

Why is it that some parents have the personality to command love and obedience, even if it is grudgingly given at times, while others get only passive compliance or rebellion? The reason, in good part, is that the art of talking is perfected by one and not by the other. In the first instance the child's heart and intelligence are reached. In the second instance, his will is set against his parents'.

Talking your child into doing what you want him to do is not excessively difficult if you are sure of yourself, if you love the child, if you are reasonable and if you follow through on your permissions or prohibitions. One boy I know had a tough father but always said of his Dad, "He's tough. But he's fair. He's never mean. He loves me. And once in a while he confides that he made a mistake. What more can I ask?"

FOUR POINTS TO CONSIDER
WHEN YOUR CHILD DATES

You have the right—in fact, the moral duty—to outline the reasonable rules under which your teen-ager begins his first serious association with the opposite sex. You are charged by God to protect him. In making these rules, which are nothing more than intelligent safeguards, it is naturally better if you discuss them reasonably with him and point out why the experience of older people makes them desirable. If he is convinced that these safeguards are necessary for his own protection, he will be more inclined to abide by them. But whether he likes the rules or not, you should enforce them.

Before allowing your child to go out on a date, you should satisfy yourself on four basic points: *Who, What, When, Where.* Let us consider these four W's in detail.

Who? This is obviously the most important question of all: With whom will your child be going? Adolescents are deeply concerned about what their companions think of them, and are eager to conform to the standards of their group. You can observe this tendency in the way they all dress alike, wear the same type of shoes, slacks and socks, comb their hair the same way, even prefer and dislike the same foods. If your son is a member of a "wild" group, chances are that he will conduct himself according to the standards of that group. Similarly, if he associates with boys and girls who by their conduct show themselves to be right-thinking and clean-living, chances also are that he will adopt similar standards.

This fact has been brought out by numerous surveys among young people themselves. Asked to list the most important moral influences in their lives, a majority cite companions ahead of their parents' example and the teachings of their Church. We do not believe this is quite true in the long run, but it indicates that one's companions can be an important influence indeed.

You should always know who your child's companions are. If your daughter is going out on a date, her escort should call for her at your home and give you an opportunity to meet him. You should tell him, as well as your daughter, what time you want her to be brought home.

"Safer" dates are generally those between members of

the same age and social groups. Prudence suggests that
there is something unusual when, for example, a young
man of twenty-five dates a girl of sixteen, or a boy of
eighteen begins seeing a young woman of twenty-three.
Such combinations generally indicate one of three things:
That the younger party is advanced intellectually or emotionally quite a bit beyond his or her age; that the older
one is unusually retarded; or that their strongest interest
in common is probably that of sex.

A parent may also be justified in wondering what is
going on when a young person from one social level begins
dating on another level considerably higher or lower. It
has been the practice of many boys from wealthier parts
of town to date girls from the "other side of the tracks,"
apparently thinking that if they seduce poor girls it is not
as bad as if they seduce one of their own social class.

The varieties of such unusual combinations are many
and must be dealt with delicately. Take the question of
dating between Catholics and non-Catholics. Everyone
knows that some mixed marriages are more successful
than some Catholic marriages and that in the existential
order it is better to marry a responsible non-Catholic than
a Catholic who is irresponsible. These are sociological facts,
and yet a Catholic parent must be alive to the truth that
the mixed marriage as an institution is a great threat to
happiness and to the Catholic faith of most people who
enter it. It is also a fact that the mixed marriage is the most
unhappy marriage in the United States if one judges only
by the statistics on divorces and separations. And it is a
fact that as many as one third of these marriages occur
without benefit of priest and that more than a third of the
children born of mixed unions are brought up without any
religion.

The difficulty is that once people are emotionally involved, the problem cannot be discussed. Everyone in love

thinks he can beat any odds. And parents who themselves look back on a victory of this kind sometimes are little inclined or in a poor position to give an objective picture of the mixed marriage situation. They are like the woman who insisted on pushing her sixteen-year-old daughter into an unwise marriage with the argument, "I was married at sixteen," apparently caring little that the other sixteen-year-olds who married with her have a high ratio of marital misery.

The only way to look at the mixed marriage is in terms of Christian history. Christ calls a man and woman to a Sacrament and for the supernatural work of producing saints. This vocation ideally needs complete unity of faith, which is absent in the mixed marriage. The subtle effect of family life in a mixed marriage, even when it has endured, is that religion and faith are not so important after all. The whole Christian education of children suffers when parents do not agree on what life and marriage is all about. This does not mean that two Catholic parents, one of whom is lax, would agree either. But again, we are speaking only of ideals.

If the child early in adolescence is educated to see a full faith as important to a really good marriage, then the Catholic religion well practiced will be as important to him when choosing a mate as, for example, pleasant personality, emotional stability, good looks or economic security. And so when he begins to date he has religion and the importance of religion uppermost in his mind. Parents, too, when they see a child sliding into a mixed dating relationship, will be in a better position to exercise good leadership. If the matter has never been discussed, the success of proper guidance will be impaired, particularly if the child, already unduly hostile to parental control, uses courtship with a non-Catholic as another instrument of defiance.

In the next few years parents will have to face the increasing prospect of interracial dating and interracial marriages. It is good for them to begin with the knowledge that no prescription of theology or canon law stands in the way of such a marriage. In this, as in all other matters of such kind, the important considerations will be the success and stability of the marriage and the proper education of the children, rather than the color of the skin. Parents in the United States easily become upset at the possibility of their son or daughter marrying someone of another race. Because of bigotry rather than religion, they create such an atmosphere of conflict in the home that the problems of the interracial marriage, which are many indeed, are never adequately discussed, particularly when the child is using this possibility to shock his parents. It is incumbent on such fathers and mothers to discuss the matter peacefully among themselves and, if they have misgivings, meet the child with reasons based on other than religious arguments.

What? The things your youngster will be doing on his date may have an important bearing on whether or not he will be subjected to temptations. For example, a date to go to the high-school basketball game and to stop in for a soda later at the village ice cream parlor would normally be about as free from temptation as one could get. On the other hand, a date at a drive-in movie theater would usually be considered quite risky. These theaters are widely known as "passion pits" because they provide a kind of protected privacy for those who engage in heavy necking, petting and intercourse itself. Even if your youngster is completely innocent himself, the fact that he attends drive-ins with a girl may well be the beginning of a tempestuous relationship.

When? During the years that a son or daughter lives

with parents the parents retain the right to influence and supervise the comings and goings of their children. Every family is different in matters such as this. But certainly youngsters under twenty-one, free to roam the highways and byways of a town, or to return home whenever their fancy suits them, may well find that the lack of a curfew is an open invitation to irresponsible conduct of one kind or another.

While most adolescents will accept without question the principle that their parents have a right to set a time to return home, there may be some disagreement about what the hour should be. Naturally, circumstances will dictate your answer. The customs of the place will suggest some norms, e.g., no one dates during the work or school week, those of certain ages must be home by 10 P.M., others are permitted out on week ends till midnight, and so forth. When their children attend dances or parties, many parents reason that the time of return should be a set hour after the affair ends. This generally provides enough time for a hamburger and coffee at a diner and the trip home. If your community has lax standards, you may have to stand against the crowd.

Where? A good general principle is that unmarried people should not go to places where they have absolute privacy—where there is nothing to stop them if desire should overtake them.

Dates or parties at private homes at which no adults are present are possible occasions of sin for young people. One girl, a high-school junior, took baby-sitting jobs on week-end nights and invited her boy friend to the homes where she was sitting, in order, she said, to listen to the radio and study with him. One night the parents who employed her unexpectedly returned home early and found her and her boy friend in a compromising position on the sofa. The girl's parents were shocked when they heard about it—but they should have known better than to allow their daughter to enter a situation where there would be no protection for her.

At the edge of one town, a tavern suddenly became very popular with some teen-agers, primarily because the proprietor was willing to sell beer and even hard liquor to persons under the legal drinking age. He also operated "tourist cabins" a few hundred feet away from his tavern. Some youngsters drank enough alcohol at the tavern to lose all their inhibitions and then rented cabins for an hour or so. At least half a dozen pregnancies of high-school girls developed from this setting before police clamped down.

Places of this kind should be out of bounds for all youngsters, even those who may have innocent intentions. It is a fact of human nature, with which we must all live, that people often are judged by appearances. The girl or boy who goes to places frequented by persons of loose morals will emerge with a tarnished reputation, whether deserved or not.

THE TWIN DANGERS OF
DRINKING AND PARKING

The practices of drinking and parking in secluded places deserve special mention. These are two additional cases in which young people are denied the special protections which existed in earlier times.

In European cultures, until recently, the idea that drinking should form the main diversion at social gatherings was generally frowned upon. People drank on social occasions, of course, but almost always as an accompaniment to other things. The drinking was usually secondary. Even today, in many parts of Europe, drinking without eating is rarely done. When a survey was made of Italian college students who regularly took wine with their meals, a great number said that they did not drink, so deeply ingrained was their idea that wine is a beverage like milk or coffee.

In the United States, the British Isles and increasingly throughout other countries of the Western world, however, drinking has become an end in itself. Extensive advertising makes it appear that the cocktail and highball are indulged in by the "best people" at any hour of the day or night.

Young people are attracted by the alluring, grown-up practice of drinking. So much so, in fact, that the carton of beer or bottle of whiskey are regarded by some as a necessary adjunct to any social gathering any place.

Unfortunately, young people lack the experience to know just how potent a force alcohol can be. They do not realize that it serves to release all inhibitions and that it distorts the judgment. What a person would not think of doing in his sober moments somehow becomes, under the influence of alcohol, a highly desirable thing to do.

Nor do they know that the effects of alcohol are highly unpredictable and depend to a great extent upon a person's immediate nervous condition, how much food he has in his stomach, how much sleep he has had the night before, and so on. Two drinks which may have little effect at one time may make a person "tight" and utterly unable to think straight at another. As a result, young people who drink on dates are literally playing with dynamite, for they have no way of knowing at what stage in their drinking they may lose their power to judge between right and wrong.

In modern life, it is ordinarily impossible for parents to prohibit their nineteen- or twenty-year-olds from attending social affairs where drinks will be served. It is probably impossible even in those areas where laws try to prohibit the sale of alcoholic beverages to minors. But if your youngster attends social events where alcoholic beverages are available, you should make sure that there are other safeguards—preferably the presence of a responsible adult nearby, and the lack of opportunity for individual couples to go off to secluded places by themselves for long periods.

Having the use of an automobile also may tempt young people on a date. The car is a means of going quickly to some isolated place, and is also a place in itself where intercourse may occur. This is not to say that young people should not use cars, but prudence suggests that parents pay close attention to how the cars are used.

If drinking and the free use of an automobile are moral hazards on dates, they are doubly or triply so when taken together. One could not begin to imagine the losses of virtue that have occurred when young people have had several drinks, and then stopped to park in a sheltered spot afterwards. The hazards involved in this combination of drinking and parking are even greater than the physical dangers of accidents from driving under the influence of alcohol. Parents would do well, therefore, to refuse to let their youngster use the family car on dates if any drinking is to be done.

CULTIVATE YOUR CHILD'S CONFIDENCE

During your child's dating days, you will find that your relationship will be much smoother if you can get him to tell you voluntarily what he has done on dates, or plans to do. If until now you have expressed genuine interest in his activities—results of school games and contests he engaged in, things he saw and did during school outings, news about his friends' comings and goings—you will have established a firm foundation of confidence. He will be more interested in you when you have continuing interest in him. It will come easier for him to talk to you about his dates when you have more than his dates in common.

Some youngsters develop a reluctance to discuss with their parents their relations with the opposite sex. This is caused by more than shyness. It is rather natural, and part of a surging independence. But if you have always assured your child of a tolerant, appreciative and understanding hearing, sooner or later you will become privy to his secrets, even earlier to hers. It will probably serve you just as well, however, if you do not make it transparent that you only want to play cop. Some parents defeat their own purposes by trying to pry out every detail from the child. When he reacts naturally by trying to avoid answers, they become as irritating as a prosecuting attorney.

Your best approach will be a gentle, understanding but authoritative one. If your youngster is doing things which are potentially harmful, you will of course point out the risks—always criticizing the act rather than the child, however.

When one mother finds it necessary to criticize something her daughter has said or done on a date, she always presages her remarks like this: "I know that you almost always handle things in the right way, Mary, but in this case, I can't help thinking that something different might have been done or said." Mary does not feel that she is under attack. Her ego—which teen-agers find it important to protect—is not directly brought into the discussion.

Another mother uses her daughter's experiences to recount her own memories of dating. She does this for two reasons: to let her daughter know that the problems and situations arising between boys and girls have not changed greatly over the years, and also to let her know that she now is grateful to her own parents for seeing to it that her virtue was protected.

Many parents have learned that the most effective way of gaining a child's confidence is to wait until the child himself is ready to talk. For example, parents of teen-agers know that at times they are moody and uncommunicative and must be prodded to answer innocent and innocuous questions. But at other times they will volunteer a full account of their doings as long as the parent will listen. If the parent keeps the lines of communication open and is patient, the child will talk eventually, and a full account is likely to be forthcoming.

BOYS ARE NOT GIRLS

While the physical growth of the adolescent is reasonably obvious, the development inside the boy or girl is far more radical. Parents may fear it difficult to handle a son who towers over them, but it is the soul of the teen-ager with which it is most difficult to deal, the girl's as well as the boy's.

We must honestly recognize, for example, that nature has made most boys body-conscious. During puberty the young man is far more sensual than his sister of similar age. He wants to be strong and to flex his muscles. He admires power and the powerful. His ideals are courage and heroism. Part of the reason Don Bosco was so successful with youth, apart from his holiness, was that he could walk on a tightrope, swallow fire, pull teeth and play musical instruments. In the male adolescent, therefore, the fighting spirit plays an important role in muscular development. This is why premature mingling of the sexes is dangerous. It stifles this growth by inclining the boy too early to assimilate qualities that are feminine, e.g., sentimentality.

Obviously, he is going to wrestle with the flesh, but it would be a mistake to have him believe that failures in this area involve him in the greatest of all vices. There are other Commandments meriting attention over and above the Sixth. And the appeal for chastity must be directed towards his natural appetite for mastery over himself. This is why mothers sometimes are seriously wrong in telling their sons: "Now be a good boy. I want my boy to be nice and innocent." This approach will repel him. Nor would a father be any more correct in educating his son this way: "Remember, son, only a low type of animal lets his passions get the better of him." This is not true.

It is better to give him a Christian view of the value of his body: In baptism, his body was joined to the Mystical Body of Our Lord; in Confirmation, his body was anointed as a Temple of the Holy Spirit; in Holy Communion, he is closely united with the Eucharistic Body of Christ; at the Anointing of the Sick, his body is readied for Redemption. His dead body will be blessed by the Church and put to rest in consecrated ground to await the Resurrection, when it becomes like the Glorified Body of the Savior.

The young man must be directed to love more than himself, and must understand that to develop the capacity for good love he needs the help of God. At the proper time, for example, association with a chaste girl will be the inspiration he needs to develop his own chastity.

Whereas the adolescent boy is sensual, the adolescent girl is sensitive. This is not to say that the sex urge is not present; but normally it is much weaker. It becomes active and alive only after her first experience with orgasm. All her other feelings for a boy, however, can be very deep. As natural as her modesty and virginity may be, she, like every woman, is made to be a mother. She wants to give herself to someone and to make sacrifices for him. In this she finds contentment and completion. A good girl can win ascendancy over even the most unruly boy. She can curb him when his own parents have despaired of doing so. And parents of adolescent girls ought to make sure that they make their daughters realize that success as women comes, not in imitating boys, but by being different.

Unless she is properly trained for her role well in advance, the young girl can make two serious mistakes: First, letting her emotions run away with her to the point of loving someone unworthy of her and about whose unworthiness she remains unconvinced until she suffers tragedy. A wise old man once said: "You can talk a woman into some things rather easily. But you never talk her out of anything." How many foolish young marriages are explained by these words. Secondly, she frequently has no understanding of her effect on the passions of a young man. How many arguments one has with teen-age girls over necking, petting, soul-kissing! Girls tell you there can be nothing wrong because they feel nothing. How naïve they are some pregnant, unmarried girl will explain very well.

These considerations ought to be part of mother-daughter talks by the time the girl is sixteen and before the girl is emotionally attached. And they are more important today than ever, when your daughter is being told in hundreds of ways that she really is not substantially different from boys and is just as much entitled to the same sexual activity as her male counterparts. Some recent studies of college students on secular campuses have shown that the girls now are far more desirous of premarital relations than the young men! And much of this is the result of the basic conviction that they must prove that they are equal to men. The idea that the woman is an exemplar to an impatient young man is vanishing in certain segments of the American culture.

Girls, therefore, ought to be encouraged to develop their femininity and motherliness, in their reception of Holy Communion to identify personally with the manhood in Christ, and to adopt His Virgin Mother as their model and support.

TEACHING THE CONSEQUENCES OF INTERCOURSE

When your child begins to date, you must face the fact that his having sexual intercourse is a possibility. There is no reason to be an extremist about this. The possibility is certainly very slight when all that is involved is a date to a school dance and a soda afterwards. On the other hand, the possibility is quite a bit greater if the youngsters involved are going out alone, engage in heavy necking as a matter of course, and are going where they will be undisturbed for several hours.

You should not worry excessively about intercourse in the first example cited above. Neither should you blithely assume that nothing serious will happen in the second instance because the boy and girl involved come from good families. The power of passion in young people does not respect the size of their parents' social position.

Premarital intercourse probably is more talked about today than at any time in Christian history. One reason for this is the breakdown in moral standards regarding sex and the widespread idea that it is a game anyone can play. Like the rest of us, teen-agers are well aware that many moderns regard intercourse much the same as they regard eating. They will engage in it anywhere, at any time, and with anybody. Of course, the only protection against this kind of thinking is a firm understanding of what sex is all about: Why God created it, and why He expects us to use it in an extremely careful way. In the last analysis, your child will resist the ever-present temptations of the times only if he has received adequate training in chastity.

What you have taught him in his youngest days about the place of sex in God's master plan, and the way you have strengthened his ability to say No to his less noble impulses, will now determine to a large extent how successful he will be in observing the Sixth Commandment during his dating and courtship days.

THE RISK OF PREGNANCY

In addition to the teachings of religion that sex outside marriage is sinful, two other pressures were exerted in earlier days. These were fear of detection—the risk that premarital intercourse would make the girl pregnant—and fear of the diseases of syphilis and gonorrhea.

Both of these deterrents have been greatly weakened in modern times—mistakenly, as we shall see. Many persons believe that artificial contraceptives have taken the risk of pregnancy out of intercourse, and that so-called miracle drugs have reduced the once-dread venereal disease to nothing more serious than the common cold. Both of these current beliefs are grave errors, however—and it would be well to let your youngsters realize that pregnancy and disease are still highly possible results of sexual promiscuity.

Let us consider the first myth that has been carefully fostered that modern contraceptives are "safe" and that users run little or no risk of pregnancy. The appalling and rising statistics on illegitimate births and abortions all over the world belie this belief. For example, a spokesman for the British Medical Association says that two out of every five babies born to girls twenty years old or younger are conceived outside of marriage, and that one birth in six is illegitimate.

It is worth noting that even in those countries where contraceptives are not only freely distributed and sold, but are even widely advocated by the government, they have proved ineffective. Japan is a country with one of the most liberal attitudes toward contraceptives in the world. Yet, despite the ready availability of devices of this kind, and a propaganda campaign to encourage the public to use them, approximately one out of every two pregnancies in Japan is an unwanted one. The woman in the case, presumably after having used contraceptives unsuccessfully, then resorts to legalized abortion.

In Red China, where there are few or no moral scruples against the use of such devices, the Communist government has, in effect, admitted that artificial methods do not achieve the results intended. The Communist rulers have undertaken a massive campaign to encourage young people to keep down the birth rate by deferring marriage until they are older. Thus they recognize that the only effective way to prevent childbirth is by abstaining from intercourse.

It might be well to mention these things to your teen-agers. The pragmatic argument that the use of contraceptives is no protection against pregnancy has sometimes proved effective in discouraging youngsters from sexual experimentation when they might not be restrained by moral considerations. The fact is that today—just as in earlier days—the person who engages in intercourse runs a very real risk of causing a pregnancy.

THE RISING VD RATES

Also subject to correction is the widespread myth that "wonder drugs" have virtually wiped out syphilis and gonorrhea, the old-time scourges of those who engaged in sex promiscuously. For instance, the Chief of the Venereal Disease Research Laboratory of the United States Public Health Service recently declared that syphilis is being reported with increasing frequency throughout the country. During 1962 there were 124,000 cases reported, including more than 21,000 in the infectious, transmissible stages. Significantly, the number of cases in which the disease could easily be given to others was the greatest number reported in a dozen years. Nor is that the worst of it. This expert, Dr. M. Brittain Moore, Jr., estimated that as many as 1,200,000 cases are not recorded. In Britain and Western Europe, the situation is similar. Dr. Ernest Claston, assistant secretary of the British Medical Association, has said that within the past ten years there has been a 45 per cent increase in the number of persons attending venereal disease clinics for the first time.

The appalling thing about the resurgence of syphilis is that most of such cases are now reported among teen-agers —and that the number of cases among those under twenty has risen sharply each year since the end of World War II.

It is probably true that a generation or two ago, parents sometimes painted such a grim and terrifying picture of pregnancy or loathsome disease as being the possible consequences of premarital intercourse that their children came to look upon sex, even inside of marriage, as something repulsive. As a result of such excessively grim warnings, some young men and women probably were never able to bring to the act of married love the sense of spontaneity and respect for its sacred character that it deserves.

I would agree that the parent who continually associates

pregnancy or syphilis with intercourse in talking to youngsters is not preparing them to view this act in its true perspective. On the other hand, it is also a mistake to go to the other extreme and to give the impression that no serious practical consequences can result from intercourse outside of marriage. You would properly warn a young automobile driver that drinking while driving is dangerous, that driving in excess of reasonable speeds increases the risk of fatal accidents, that other serious damage can result from failure to observe safety precautions. A similar statement of facts and figures regarding the dangers of sexual promiscuity may convince your youngster that, despite what secular influences may sometimes indicate, it can be fraught with consequences that will last a lifetime.

APPEALS TO IDEALISM ARE EFFECTIVE

Appeals to a young person's idealistic concepts of parenthood often carry great weight, too. Your child has seen how much concentrated effort you have put into his upbringing. He realizes that you have spent countless hours on his behalf—devoting yourself almost entirely to his care when he was an infant, sitting with him for hours when he was ill, spending inestimable amounts of time in teaching and encouraging skills like walking and feeding himself, and countless hours more in the sheer physical effort of preparing his meals and cleaning up after them, in making his bed, washing and mending his clothes, and cleaning his room. He knows that parenthood is a full-time job.

In addition, every youngster has a strong sense of responsibility toward those younger than himself. Even hardened criminals hesitate to give a bad example in front of children. All of us realize that we should be on our good behavior with the young, lest we scandalize the "little ones" of Our Lord.

What does all of this mean? It means that when you suggest to a young person that premarital intercourse may result in the birth of a baby who will have no one old enough, wise enough and capable enough to take care of him, you are presenting an argument that cannot be refuted. At the same time you are appealing to his idealism.

MAKE YOUR CHILD MORALLY SELF-RELIANT

At some late stage of your child's adolescent development, you probably will have to reach some definite conclusion as to how much responsibility you yourself must carry for his spiritual condition. In the past, parents were prone to put the entire responsibility on the child and to accept none of the guilt themselves if the child committed serious sin. This type of thinking gave rise to the stereotype of the father throwing his daughter out of the house upon discovering that she had sinned against the Sixth Commandment. Most of us now realize that such an attitude is hard, unfeeling, and above all, un-Christian.

Insofar as a child reflects his parents' teaching and example, a father and mother cannot feel themselves entirely without burden if their child makes some serious mistakes. It sometimes happens that parents too easily acquiesce to the underage marriage of their son or daughter, particularly when their legal permission is necessary. Because a teenager insists on making a fool of himself is no reason why the parent, particularly the father, need endorse this foolishness.

On the other hand, it is an error to believe that parents bear the major guilt for anything their child may do. Too many psychotherapists today will hold parents responsible for every transgression that a child commits. If you will look back again upon your own childhood and adolescence, you will realize how preposterous this notion is. How many times in your own developing years did you hold the power in your own hands to resist temptation or yield to it? How many times did you alone, through your own free will, make a deliberate choice between remaining in a state of grace or departing from it? All of us probably experienced thousands of situations in which the decision to do right or wrong rested entirely with ourselves.

You must remember that your child has his own personality and his own free will, and that your direct influence over him when he reaches his late teens is limited. We are fortunate that this is so. Otherwise we would all be robots in patterns laid down for us by our forebears, and improvement in the human race would be out of the question. The child of sinful or indifferent parents would have no hope of rising above his spiritual condition. He would be doomed from his very first day to a pattern of life identical to theirs.

We do not accept this deterministic point of view, nor do we believe a human being is like a cork bouncing on the sea, carried this way or that by every wave. Rather, we believe that every human being has power to rise above his environment, power to resist evil influences which may exist all around him. This does not mean that a child will not be greatly influenced by the examples of his parents, the environment in which he lives and other factors. Nevertheless, he has the power through his own free will to rise above his station and lead a life of sanctity. Believing this, we must also believe its opposite—that the child exposed to the good example of his parents and countless opportunities to live in a state of grace may choose to move in the direction of evil.

Parents of eighteen- or nineteen-year-olds may profit from the story of the self-starter. When automobiles first came on the scene, their owners had to get in front of them, and had to turn a hand-crank vigorously for minutes, in order to get the car motors started. Later, self-starters were invented. Drivers merely pressed a button and within a few seconds the motor was running smoothly.

You must crank up your young child to get him moving in the direction you want him to go. You teach him all about God and the difference between right and wrong; you supervise his physical development, see that he eats proper food, gets enough sleep, and is dressed properly and protected against the cold.

By the time he has finished high school, however, you should be able to throw the crank away. Now he must start himself. He must take the responsibility upon himself to lead a good Christian life, to obey the Commandments, to frequent the Sacraments.

Of course, with your car, you try to provide conditions that will enable the self-starter to work. You make sure that the battery has plenty of water. You keep the car in the garage on cold nights, so that the motor will not get too cold and be difficult to start in the morning.

Likewise, you should provide a good environment for your child. You will be doing this if you are leading a Christian life and fulfilling the requirements of the Commandments yourself. But when you have provided the conditions that will enable the normal self-starter to function properly, you have to let it work.

Taking spiritual responsibility is something he must learn for his own welfare, for just as today's car owner has no way of cranking the car if the self-starter won't work, so too the time will come when your children will have no one to crank them up—when they must either start themselves or find themselves stalled for life.

What then would be the best attitude for a parent? You should realize that, in the final analysis, you are responsible to God for your own conduct. Regardless of the influences for good or evil to which you yourself have been subjected during your lifetime, you alone must answer to God for the life you have lived. On the Day of Judgment you will be unable to pass the responsibility onto anyone else. So, too, your children must answer for themselves in the light of the life they themselves have chosen to live. We can believe that a merciful God will forgive much more from the child who has been exposed to evil influences all his life than from one who has turned his back on the good teachings and examples he received during his formative years. Yet it is a basic part of Christian belief that each individual is responsible for his own salvation.

Although your child will be subjected to God's last judgment on the basis of what he himself has done with his life, you cannot wash your hands of the entire matter. For on your own Day of Judgment, you will have to account for what you did with the child God placed in your care. Did you do your best to teach him to know, love and serve God and to respect His Commandments? Did you set a good example? Did you do your best to help him spiritually?

WHEN YOUR CHILD LIVES
AWAY FROM HOME

More and more youngsters of eighteen or so are leaving home for at least part of the year, and going where they no longer will be subject to their parents' direct influence. They go off to college, to the armed forces, to take jobs in other parts of the country for the summer, or to set up their own households even though they are unmarried.

Obviously, when your child is on his own, he will have greater freedom to act as he pleases. In some cases it is fairly certain he will do things away from home that he would never dare do if his parents were keeping watch over him.

There is no denying the fact that temptations will increase greatly when he is away from home—even when he is at a college under religious supervision. Given the relaxed moral standards of the times and the innumerable opportunities offered to young people today, it is unrealistic to believe that temptations will not arise. You can only hope that at this stage he will show the moral stamina and adherence to moral principles you have tried to inculcate.

Because you cannot protect your child as much as you could heretofore, this does not mean that you should do nothing. If your child is going away to college, you should make every effort to see that he lives in a dormitory under supervision, or at least lives in a home near the college where adherence to regular hours and acceptable behavior will be required.

Parents often still control the purse strings at this time, and they should not give their youngsters carte blanche to use their allowances for dubious purposes. For example, paying for week ends where there will be free mingling of the sexes away from chaperones is an open invitation to riotous behavior. Anyone who doubts this might question the managers of New York hotels where college students have been in the habit of staying during long week ends, end-of-term vacations, and the like. Drinking to the point of blacking out is one of the lesser things that happens regularly.

While you rightly might be concerned about the influences to which your youngster is exposed, it is well to remember that your son or daughter must spend the rest of his life in a culture that includes ways of life other than his own. You cannot isolate him indefinitely. Sooner or later, he must face the fact that sex is everywhere, that a large segment of the population believes that sex was made for recreation, and that many think that sexual indulgence is necessary for good health. Your youngster will have to decide that Christian values are more important to him than anything else, and that no happiness can be found in the unrestrained submission to passion. He must have an intellectual basis for believing that sexual indulgence before marriage is sinful and can cause much greater worldly anguish and heartaches than whatever pleasure may be derived from it. He must have a solid understanding of the fact that in exercising control over himself and his sexual desires, he is establishing the only basis for a sound and happy life in later years.

What you taught your child in his earlier years will now bear fruit. It is now when your teaching him to discipline himself and to say No to desires passing through his mind will enable him to resist the temptations which press in on him. And it is now when he will have the courage to stand against the crowd knowingly and positively, because of the conviction you have given him that he should do what is right whether his action is approved by few or by many.

THE WAYWARD CHILD

What can parents do if, despite their own teaching and example, their older teen-ager or young adult seems to persist in a sinful relationship outside of marriage? Unfortunately, this question is being asked more often these days, thanks to the propaganda flooding in from all sides that says that there is "something beautiful" about the sexual act when "two people love each other," whether they are married or not. Also widespread is the false belief that a man and woman are entitled to special privileges, including even intercourse, as soon as they become engaged.

After a child reaches a certain age—perhaps eighteen or nineteen—there is little that parents can do to stop him if he wants to commit sin. If their teaching and example fail at this point, they can only pray that their child will sooner or later come to his senses before permanent damage is done. A heart-to-heart talk may help. But repeated lectures, recriminations, name-calling, the creation by parents of rules which they will find it impossible to enforce, all may do considerably more harm than good.

If it is the sad fact that parents can do little or nothing to stop a child hell-bent on violating the Sixth Commandment, they have a moral obligation not to do anything which might make it easier for him to sin. One father had good reason to suspect that his son was using the family car to take his girl friend to an isolated beach a few miles from town, and to have intimate relations there. The father told his son that he could not use the car after dark thereafter. A mother discovered that when her twenty-one-year-old daughter spent week ends at her girl friend's house while the friend's parents were away, they invited boys to the house, and the boys stayed overnight. This mother prohibited her daughter from staying overnight anywhere with anyone. In rare instances where an adult son or daughter persists in immoral or scandalous behavior, the father may have to offer the option of a personal reform or residence elsewhere.

THE PLACE OF SEX IN MARRIAGE

In discussing with an older child the factors that should be considered in choosing a marriage partner, you will find that it is impossible (and indeed undesirable) to divorce the question of sexual attraction from this question. In fact, such a discussion will give you the opportunity to implant some idea about the role that sex should play in marriage—and about the factors that constitute a good sexual adjustment.

Naturally, your son and daughter will want to marry someone who is attractive physically. This is as it should be, because mutual physical attraction adds zest to a marriage.

Where youngsters err, however, is in thinking that physical attraction is the most important characteristic their marriage partner should have. In thinking this, they often also tend to think that physical attractiveness in itself contributes the most to sexual happiness. This assumption is one you should strive to overcome, because the idea that a pretty girl makes the best wife and a handsome boy makes the best husband lies at the root of many broken marriages.

The fact is that the qualities of thoughtfulness, consideration, and kindness are the ones which in the final analysis contribute most to sexual compatibility, as well as to successful married life. Youngsters must realize that marriage is more than sex, and that sex is more than the mere coming together of two attractive physical bodies. They should be taught that the act of sex is primarily a spiritual and emotional experience—and two persons, no matter how physically dazzling, will be unable to achieve lasting satisfaction in marriage if they lack spiritual and emotional rapport.

Your child should come to realize that there cannot be harmony in the intimate relationships between husband and wife unless there is harmony on all levels of living. The act of sex cannot be divorced from acts of kindness performed in the kitchen or the living room, or thoughtfulness expressed in everyday living.

Try to get your children to realize that while good looks in a partner are desirable, a good character and personality are even more so. If they can learn to look for qualities that really matter—kindness, sympathy, understanding, honesty, sincerity, and above all, respect for other people and their rights—they will be given the best guide for the achieving of a good sexual adjustment in marriage. Good looks pass away—sometimes with shocking speed—but the person who is kind, sympathetic and sincerely interested in the welfare of others has qualities which are likely to last for life.

In preparing her daughter for marriage, a conscientious mother would teach something about cooking, sewing and homemaking. She would rightly feel that she was helping her daughter to fulfill her role as a wife and homemaker. It is a fact, however, that a wife's ability to give her husband joy in their marital relationship may be a more important factor in cementing her marriage than any proficiency she displays in the kitchen. For it would certainly seem true that when husband and wife both achieve a great sense of satisfaction from their moments of greatest intimacy their bond will be greatly strengthened.

WHAT OLDER TEEN-AGERS SHOULD KNOW

Because youngsters in their late teens and early twenties often tend to talk big and to pretend to know everything, even in areas in which they are actually very ignorant, parents often assume that the children know a great deal more about sex than they really do. However, anyone who has talked at length with young people on this subject is usually impressed with the vast gaps in their knowledge.

Recently a college professor asked his sophomore students to define the word adultery. He discovered that two thirds of his students could not give a reasonably accurate definition. In view of such experiences, it is easy to see why parents sometimes greatly overestimate their youngsters' knowledge. In this area, it might be well to adopt the principle not to overestimate how much your child knows, nor to underestimate his desire to do the right thing once the moral law is explained to him.

Nor does the fact that young people know something about the anatomical aspects of sex mean that they really understand the subject. They may have some idea about the relative positions of men and women in intercourse and the way the organs come together. But they themselves realize that this knowledge is not enough. They want to know more about the spiritual and emotional significance of the sexual act. When doctors discuss this subject with young engaged couples, they find that the young men and women are relatively uninterested in the techniques of intercourse. They are much more interested in the attitudes that husbands and wives bring to the act.

In talking with your own youngsters who are thinking of marriage, you will probably find that they are anxious to learn about the specific roles they are expected to play as husband or wife. So much is made these days about the equality of the sexes that young people should fully realize that there is a vast difference between men and women in their physical and emotional make-up. Unless they know this—and apply their knowledge—a good sexual adjustment will be difficult, if not impossible.

Some women object to the introduction of this idea. They fail to make a distinction between equality and difference. Two things may have equal value, yet they are different. For example, the English pound may be worth $2.80 in U.S. money. Thus the pound and $2.80 are equal—yet no one can deny that they are different. An Englishman with nothing but pounds in his purse will find that shopkeepers in America will refuse to take his money for their merchandise.

The importance of bridegrooms understanding their brides, and vice versa, cannot be stressed too strongly. For understanding is the first step to accepting—and unless a husband can understand the fundamental nature of the woman he marries, he will find himself continually frustrated as he undertakes the impossible task of turning her into a woman with the characteristics of a man. Consider how these differences relate to sex. A man by nature is aroused very easily. He is subject to arousal sometimes if he sees a photograph of an undraped woman. He may get a whiff of perfume, and immediately start thinking of sex. His wife may toss her head in a certain way, or throw him a glance, and desire may well up within him. On the other hand, his wife's desires will not be awakened so easily, as a general thing. She might go for a long time—perhaps even many months—without feeling a strong urge for sex while her husband might experience strong desires after a few days.

A wife's desires may often stem from emotional rather than physical causes. An act of unexpected kindness from her husband, an evening when he has gone out of his way to treat her like a duchess, a charitable act he may have performed for someone else—any number of things like these may set the stage for her emotionally. Unless she has this emotional desire, intercourse loses much of its value for her.

When a husband and wife understand even these differences in their natures, they will be able to accept more readily many day-by-day experiences. It will not shock a wife to discover that her husband seeks intercourse almost as a spur-of-the-moment impulse. Nor will a husband's ego be shattered if his wife sometimes finds it impossible to respond enthusiastically to his advances.

As your child gets ready for marriage, then, you can be most constructive if you talk to him about the basic roles which must be played by wives and husbands. Fathers should take their sons aside and talk to them openly about what is expected of the husband: That it is a man's function to initiate love and teach his wife. If the young man has a good picture of his responsibilities, he will treat his bride sensitively, with a great deal of kindness and patience. A mother should instruct her daughter on the responsibility of a wife.

These talks might emphasize that a couple's sexual relationship often reflects their whole relationship and reveals how they react to each other in the other areas of their lives. This being so, the husband who always strives to treat his wife gently, with consideration and good-natured acceptance, is the one most likely to make a good adjustment sexually.

Young people must learn that selfless consideration of the other partner's needs is the key to true love, and that the same spirit of selflessness is necessary for a good adjustment in the marriage bed. Each individual must learn to keep selfish desires in check and to put concern for the partner ahead of one's own wants.

Suppose, for example, that a husband is anxious for frequent intercourse and has no concern for the fact that such frequency may not be satisfying to his wife. He may be inclined to make her something of a plaything, and while he may achieve satisfaction for himself, his wife will achieve little or none.

On the other hand, the wife who thinks intercourse should be indulged in only when she herself wants it, and disregards her husband's wants, will not inspire a true sense of companionship, because she is also using sex as a one-sided vehicle for her own desires. And there also are times when both persons may wish to engage in intercourse but must refrain from doing so, so that a greater good— something bigger than both of them—may be gained.

In discussing these matters with the bride-to-be or bridegroom-to-be in your family, you might well stress that there will be many times when the rights of the other party, and circumstances beyond the control of both of them, will make it necessary for one or both persons to practice self-restraint. Such times would be when one partner is physically or emotionally indisposed and unable to engage in the act; when there are aesthetic objections by one or both partners, as for example when the wife is menstruating; and during the period in the wife's cycle when intercourse might result in a baby which for good reasons the couple think they should not bring into the world.

The point we are making is that young people often believe that when they are married, they can engage in an unlimited amount of sex. The truth is otherwise. From almost the first day of marriage, they will have to regulate themselves.

Try, therefore, to teach your son or daughter to think in terms of chastity from the very beginning. As I have mentioned before, chastity is the virtue which keeps sex in its proper place. It is as important for a husband to be chaste when his wife cannot have intercourse as it is for any unmarried person to be chaste. This is a vital piece of information for a young man to have. And it is as necessary for husband and wife to refrain from intercourse which might result in a baby they do not want as it is for single persons to refrain at all times.

Some persons argue that if they must avoid having a baby, it is too much to expect them to forego intercourse during the four or five days each month when the possibility of conception exists. Of course, this argument says in effect that there is no place for will power. It also ignores the fact that most couples have intercourse to a greater extent than they really need, just as most of us tend to eat more than we need to maintain good health. Experience teaches that almost any couple can abstain for longer periods than they think possible, without causing any emotional or physical harm. It is possible for couples to refrain for longer periods—many weeks and months and sometimes even years—when they have a true spiritual motivation for doing so. All things are possible with the grace of the Sacraments which are not possible without them.

Do not underestimate the idealism of young people and their ability to rise to a challenge which demands heroic sacrifices. These words of Pope Pius XII hit the mark:

> To judge men and women of today incapable of continuous heroism is to do them wrong. In these days, for many reasons—perhaps through dire necessity or even at times to the pressure of injustice—heroism is being practiced to a degree and extent that in times past would have been thought impossible. Why then, if circumstances demand it, should this heroism stop at the limit described by passion and the inclination of nature? It is obvious that he who does not want to master himself, will not be able to do so; and he who thinks he can master himself, relying solely on his own powers and not sincerely and perseveringly seeking divine aid, will be miserably deceived.

GUIDANCE FOR THE ENGAGED

A great complaint of young men and women of marrying age is that their parents will not talk to them about sex. A survey we made of engaged couples in New York indicated that this feeling is widespread. The young men and women thought that their mothers and fathers trained them adequately for their roles as husbands and fathers, gave the boys instruction in what they must do as providers and gave the girls a good idea of what it meant to run a home. But when it came to guidance about sex, many felt let down.

Actually, it is highly unlikely that a person eighteen years of age or older does not understand what the sexual act is all about. What young people of this age want, therefore, is not so much facts about sex, but the proper attitudes toward it and some assurances that they will be able to manage successfully.

Although this has been called an age when everybody knows everything about sex, young people are often timid about the marital experiences they will encounter as bride and bridegroom. Even the youngster who displays the greatest braggadocio about such matters may desperately need guidance about the true nature of intercourse.

A father should not assume that his son knows everything simply because the son has a knowledge of the anatomical details of the act. The young man of today is not immune from a complete lack of consideration for his bride, and is perhaps as likely as newlywed husbands of earlier generations to display utter selfishness on his honeymoon.

A father should explain to his son that the act of sex is a very deep and profound experience for a bride. In this act she is literally invaded. If a man performs this act without regard for his wife's sensitivities and without preparing her emotionally and physically for this invasion, so that she is mentally and physically receptive, the experience may be a distasteful—even repulsive—one for her. Some authorities have even suggested that the husband forego marital relations on the wedding night because the bride's nervous exhaustion after the wedding ceremony itself may make her less than ready emotionally for this experience. (Most advisors, however, would not go quite this far.)

In any event, the bridegroom's father might explain to his son that thoughtful consideration of the bride's wishes should be paramount in the bridegroom's thoughts on his wedding night. Of course, most fathers would find it difficult to explain acts which a husband might legitimately engage in in order to arouse his wife's desires and make his wife eager to participate actively in coitus. The bridegroom might be encouraged to attend a series of Pre-Cana Conferences on this subject, or the father might put into his son's hands a Catholic marriage manual which explains these things with dignity. At any rate, a father should urge his son to introduce the bride to the act of sex with great delicacy, to encourage her to achieve full emotional and physical satisfaction and so to make their intimate moments ones which both can share joyfully. To a large extent, whether or not a bride has a satisfactory sexual relationship with her husband will depend upon the manner in which this relationship begins.

In a similar way, a mother should prepare her daughter who will soon become a bride. How well she does her job may have an important effect upon the attitudes her daughter brings to the marriage bed.

A marriage guide for ladies published a century ago quoted one experienced wife who said that during the sexual act she kept her mind on such matters as new curtains for the kitchen, on clothes that needed mending, or on things to buy the next time she went shopping. The belief that a good wife satisfied her husband's passionate desires but derived no satisfaction from sex herself was characteristic of those times. Of course, today's women realize that God did not make sex for men's enjoyment only.

While a modest mother may wish to refer her daughter to a Catholic marriage manual for a somewhat more detailed description of the sex act than she feels free to discuss, she can quite properly advise her daughter that it is just as moral for a wife to take pleasure from the act as it is for her husband. The wife might well engage in acts which intensify her own desire, and it is proper and desirable to express appreciation of her husband's love-making abilities. Women who are well-loved physically are delightful companions and gentle mothers.

THE QUESTION OF CONTRACEPTION

I have mentioned before the importance of giving your children a standard to govern their conduct all their lives— the standard being what God wants them to do. If they ask themselves what God wishes of them, they will be better able to decide whether or not any given conduct is really best for them from the long-term point of view.

As regards the use of contraceptives, about which your engaged son or daughter may be curious, the importance of this standard cannot be underestimated. Thanks to a widespread, insistent campaign of propaganda, advocates of artificial birth control devices often try to convey the impression that everybody who refuses to use such things is out of step. To judge from material in the press and elsewhere, one might think Catholics alone were nonusers. Even if this were so, there would be no justification for using them. God's law remains God's law, whether one person in a million obeys it, or whether everyone does. This is a point it is well to get across to your children, because it will help them realize why they *must* pursue a moral course of action in marriage, even if it be unpopular at the moment.

Long before any temptation to use contraceptives arises,

your children should be told why their use is opposed: God gave man and woman their sex organs to be used for the propagation of the human race. When contraceptives are used, they put the purpose of using sex for pleasure ahead of the purpose God intended.

Even when there are no strong religious reasons for avoiding contraceptives, many men and women have a deep, instinctual feeling against tampering with our God-given natural processes. The innate voice that tells us we should not fool around with the natural order of things is illustrated by the difficulties that developed several years ago, when the drug Thalidomide was introduced in Europe. It was promoted as a quick way of inducing sleep, and at the time few persons gave serious thought to its possible consequences in areas far removed from that for which it was recommended. Yet pregnant women who took such pills ran a serious risk of giving birth to deformed babies.

Who can say that the new oral contraceptive now being widely promoted will not have similar serious side effects that may reveal themselves ten, fifteen or twenty years from now? Dr. Herbert Ratner, Commissioner of Public Health in Oak Park, Illinois, declared that at a meeting of the Third European Congress of the International Planned Parenthood Federation, a British expert on family planning education from that organization reported on a poll taken of doctors at the World Health Organization: "No single doctor I asked would advise his daughter to use [the pill]."

"Similar expressions have been privately reported in this country," Dr. Ratner declared. "At the same meeting, Dr. Nikonchik of the USSR, during a sharp discussion on oral steroid contraceptives, stated that 'We have no right to alter the harmonious hormonal structure given by nature.' Parenthetically, it should be seen from this that the understanding of rights in God's created order is not limited to

those within the Church or to those who only believe in
God. . . .

" 'The pill' unquestionably is the most dangerous contraceptive product now on the market. It has caused deaths
and heart-breaking medical complications, and its safety is
still under investigation by the government. Because of its
alleged high acceptance rate by the indigent, a group
which has rejected other contraceptives in the past, its
dangers are being minimized. This is contributing to the
destruction of one of the great traditions of medicine:
'That physicians do not prescribe for others what they will
not prescribe for their own.' "

COURSES IN MARRIAGE

In an increasing number of dioceses, special courses are
now being conducted for the Catholic bride- and bridegroom-to-be. A typical course, or Pre-Cana Conference,
consists of three meetings at which a priest discusses the
spiritual and emotional aspects of married life, a doctor
discusses the physical relationship, and experienced husbands and wives discuss practical problems that arise in
day-to-day living. At these meetings, the young man and
woman gain a greater insight not only into the sexual aspect
of marriage but also into many other aspects which will be
reflected in the way they respond to each other in intercourse.

At a Pre-Cana Conference, the expectant bride and
bridegroom have an opportunity to ask questions which
may have puzzled them and which they have been unwilling to ask parents, relatives or friends. They can discuss
even their most intimate problems in an atmosphere of
candor and reverence for the vocation of marriage which
they plan to enter.

As one young woman explained, "Were it not for the Pre-Cana Conferences, my husband and I would have entered marriage about as blind as any two persons could be. In these meetings, we found out what marriage is all about. For the preparation for our marriage which we received, we will be eternally thankful."

How can you find out where and when Pre-Cana Conferences for brides- and bridegrooms-to-be may be held in your diocese? The best way is to look for poster announcements in the vestibule or on the bulletin board of your parish church. If that investigation fails to reveal an answer, ask your parish priest. He may refer you to the director of the Family Life Bureau of your diocese, who could answer your questions.

Where Pre-Cana Conferences have not yet been instituted, parish priests will often personally instruct expectant couples. Whether they give the instructions or you do, the important thing is that your child will enter marriage— the most momentous step of his life—with a thorough spiritual and emotional preparation.

Part Two

❦ ❦

How To Tell Your
Child About Sex

THIS is a how-to-do-it section. Many parents who want to teach know what they should say. But most are inhibited from doing their job right because they are at a loss for words. This glossary of pertinent ideas and answers to questions likely to be asked by children is intended to be a handy reference for such parents. Not that any parent runs to a book for an answer he is unprepared to give. But as his child develops, he has many moments to do background reading on subjects that eventually will come into parent-child discussions. And when he is stumped, as sometimes we all are, the intelligent parent finds the right answer quickly and artfully.

The information here is about as complete as any child needs to know, regardless of his age. It is information which you might use in answering questions which arise as a result of your child's everyday living experiences—from snatches of adult conversations he may overhear, from facts or alleged facts he may pick up from friends or classmates, from something he sees on television or reads in newspapers, books or magazines.

In the final analysis, of course, you must be the judge of how much information your child can comprehend and use properly at any given age in his development. As a general rule, however, the information contained below is suitable for all ages and could be given to a child of any age without fear that he might use the information in the wrong way.

You may find that the expanded explanation of certain subjects is entirely too detailed for the young child. You will find that a briefer explanation—which might be sufficient for your youngster—is contained in the first paragraph or two. If your child asks you about a certain subject and you feel that a detailed explanation is not warranted, you might give the information contained at the beginning and omit the remainder.

There are some subjects in this list about which your child may never ask you. Don't feel that you have to give him the information unless he requests it. The information is given here, however, in case you need it.

As mentioned in Part One, every child of six or seven years should have certain minimum information about sex, about the way babies are born, why boys and girls are different, the need for modesty, and so on. Even if your child of that age has never asked about these things, you should initiate the discussion and tell him without being asked.

A girl of eleven or twelve should clearly understand what menstruation is all about, how babies are conceived, and what development of her sexual organs means in terms of her ability to become a mother. She should also have some understanding of the obligations and responsibilities that rest upon a mother.

Before your son reaches the age of thirteen or fourteen, he should know in a general way that the sex act consists of the union of male and female and that babies are conceived as a result of this act. Just as a mother should prepare her daughter for young womanhood, a father should tell his son to expect the growth of his sex organs, the coming of hair around the pubic area, and the natural discharge of semen in his sleep throughout adolescence and until he marries.

Whether they ask about it or not, boys and girls also should be told about precautions they should take to protect their chastity when dating. They should also know the real significance of going steady. They should realize that it is a preparatory step toward marriage and should be discouraged until they are able to shoulder the responsibilities of marriage and parenthood.

As a conscientious parent, you should also undertake to instruct your son or daughter who is preparing for marriage. Your child should know the specific roles that must be played by husband and wife to make a success of marriage, and the teaching of the Church regarding contraception, abortion and sterilization.

If you give this information whether your child asks for it or not, you will be sure that you have provided at least the basic core of knowledge—the information necessary for understanding the principles God had in mind when He created sex.

As was pointed out in the first chapter, you should also be prepared to answer your child's questions as frankly as possible. Your answers need not go into great detail. Your child probably would not retain such details anyway. But you should tell him in a general way the significance of various human acts which involve sex or the sex organs, and the meaning of words commonly used in discussing parts of the body, the relationships of the sexes, pregnancy and childbirth.

ADULTERY.   A sin against the Sixth Commandment of God.

A married person who gives himself or herself completely to anyone other than his own wife or husband is called an adulterer.

AFTERBIRTH. When a baby is growing inside the mother's body, a special lining of the womb enables the mother to feed her baby and provide oxygen so he can breathe. This lining is called the placenta. After the baby is born, the placenta comes out of the mother's body, along with a membrane that enclosed the baby in the womb. These things are called the afterbirth.

ANUS. The opening of the lower end of the intestines. Waste matter from the bowels passes through it.

AREOLA. This is the brownish, circular part of the breast. The nipple is the center.

BABIES. *How they are conceived.* When God decided to make men and women, He also made a way for mothers and fathers to have babies. He decided that the father should place seeds in the mother's body. When one of the father's seeds joins and pierces the mother's egg, a baby's life is begun.

This act is performed by the father placing his penis in the mother's vagina, and leaving the seed in her body.

How they develop. A baby begins in the mother's body as a tiny cell. It is no bigger than the point you could make with a sharp pencil. God wants a baby to grow big and strong, and to be safe, so He made a special place for him to stay during the nine months or so that he grows inside the mother's body. After that time, the baby is big enough to come out and live and breathe all by himself.

God gives every mother a place inside her body called the uterus, or womb. Womb is the same word we use in the Hail Mary, when we speak of Jesus as the fruit of the Blessed Mother's womb.

As the baby starts to grow the original cell becomes two

cells, then four, then eight, then sixteen, and so on. The more and more cells there are, the bigger the baby grows. By the time he is ready to be born, he will have millions of cells—just the same as you do.

Some of the cells become part of the head, some become skin, and some become lungs and hands and heart and stomach. In his second month of life, the baby is still very tiny, only about the size of your thumb. But if you could look closely, you would see that he looks like a real baby already. He has a head with tiny eyes and ears, nose and mouth, and he has arms and legs.

He keeps growing faster and faster. At the end of four months, he is about the size of my hand. He also begins to kick his legs. Because he is getting so big, he makes his mother's body look much bigger, especially her stomach, where the baby is.

When the baby has been in the mother's body for nine months, he is about as long as the distance from my elbow to the tip of my hand. He weighs six or seven pounds or so. But he has arms and legs and eyes and ears and nose and throat and stomach, and he is ready to live outside his mother's body.

It may seem strange to think of a whole new baby inside the mother's body, but he is curled up tight. His arms and legs are curled into his body, and he's just as snug as you can imagine.

A cord is attached to a lining of the mother's uterus and it runs from the baby's navel. This cord is like a pipe. It connects the baby's blood with the mother's blood. The food the mother eats goes into her blood and then is carried to the baby's blood, so that he gets fed too, and that is what helps him to grow. And you know that everybody has to breathe oxygen to stay alive. This oxygen is in the air you breathe. The mother also breathes for her tiny baby, and the oxygen she takes into her blood is carried to the baby's blood.

How they are born. When the baby is ready to be born, the mother's uterus begins to come together little by little. In this way it pushes the baby out of her body.

This is called labor. It is really hard work. At the beginning the muscles of the uterus begin to contract every hour or so, then every half-hour. Gradually the time between the contractions grows shorter and shorter. Whenever the muscle contracts the mother feels a pain like cramps.

When she feels these pains begin, and notices that they keep coming back at regular intervals, she knows it is time for the baby to be born. Usually she has plenty of time to call her doctor, and to arrange to go to the hospital.

Most mothers have their babies in the hospital. Hospitals have all the equipment they need to make sure the mother and the baby will be safe. For example, sometimes babies are born before the end of the nine months. If they come more than a few weeks early they are called premature. The hospital has special cribs called incubators where these babies can be kept warm and can get the special attention they need, because they are not as strong as they would be if they stayed in the mother's body the full nine months.

The hospital has a place called the delivery room where mothers go just before their babies are born. Nurses and doctors there make the mothers as comfortable as they can, and give them medicine if labor pains are too much for them.

The nurses can tell exactly when the baby is moving from the mother's uterus into an opening in her body which God made to let the baby come out. The baby usually comes out head first, and the doctor is standing by to hold him. The doctor holds the baby by his legs and lifts him up, and spanks him a little bit. The reason for this is to get the baby to start crying. When the baby cries, he begins to breathe by himself, and also coughs any fluid out of his lungs that might have been caught there. The doctor cuts the cord that has attached the baby to the mother's body and has carried food and oxygen to the baby. This cord is at the baby's navel—the "belly button"—and the doctor cuts it because now the baby can breathe by himself. It does not hurt when the cord is cut, and after a while, all that remains is the navel. Everybody has one. From that time on, the baby will take food in his mouth, just as we do, and such things as moving his bowels and passing urine he will also do on his own.

Having a baby is really very hard work for the mother, because she uses muscles she has not been used to using. It takes a while for her to get back her strength. That is why she must rest and take things easy for some days after her baby is born.

While the baby was growing inside her body, the mother's breasts got larger and fuller. God gave her breasts so she could feed her baby, a special kind of milk which will make him strong enough so that after a few months he will be able to eat other foods. Then, the baby's teeth will emerge so he can eat food like meat and bread. Sometimes mothers cannot give their babies enough milk from their breasts. When that happens, special formulas are used so that the babies can get almost the some kind of food from bottles.

How their sex is determined. There is no way for mothers and fathers to tell whether they will have a baby boy or baby girl until the baby is born. Then they can tell he's a boy if he has a penis, and that she's a girl if she has a vagina.

Although there's no way to tell what the baby's sex will be before he's born, scientists know that something happens to make a boy, and something else happens to make a girl. They know that if the father's seed, or sperm, has a certain type of chromosomes, called the Y type, a baby boy will be born. If the seed has a type of chromosomes they call the X type, a girl will be born.

The father has sperm with both the X type and the Y type, and it is a question of God's will which type unites with the mother's egg to form a baby. As far as we know, there are only guesses about what a father or mother can do to make sure that they will have a boy or a girl. Fathers and mothers are very happy with any baby that God gives them.

How they get their characteristics. You'll often hear people say that so-and-so looks just like his father, or has the same eyes, nose or hair as his mother, or smiles just like his uncle. There's a good reason for this, because fathers and mothers give many of their physical characteristics to their children.

Exactly how this works, nobody really knows. But we do know that many traits are inherited. For example, if a father and mother have certain types of blood, their babies will have certain types. Blue-eyed parents will have a blue-eyed baby, and red-haired parents will probably have a red-haired baby.

But a mother and father have no control over what their babies will look like. When a baby's life is started, there is about an even chance that the baby will be a boy and an even chance that it will be a girl.

The sperm cell of the father and egg cell of the mother are so tiny they can hardly be seen. But these cells have things called chromosomes which give the family traits to the children. These are traits like color of the skin, color of the eyes, shape of the nose or other parts of the face, and so on. Tall, blond parents will probably have tall, blond children, and short, dark parents will probably have short, dark children.

Because these traits are carried on from one generation to the other, it shouldn't be a surprise if a baby doesn't look like his mother or father. He may look like his grand-mother or grandfather, or even like a great-great-grand-mother or grandfather. There are so many different combinations of traits that it is hard to say what a baby will inherit. The important thing is that a baby is *himself.* Whether he has the traits of one parent or the other, his mother and father love him just as he is, because this special combination of characteristics he has is what makes him a person different from everybody else in the world.

BAG OF WATERS.   This is a membrane full of fluid. It encloses the baby during pregnancy and serves as a shock-absorber, so that the baby won't be hurt when the mother moves about. This membrane generally bursts just before birth. Sometimes the discharge of the water is the first indication that the baby is about ready to be born.

BIRTH CONTROL.   See *Contraception.*

BODY TEMPERATURE METHOD.   See *Family Limitation.*

BOOKS.   See *Reading Matter.*

BREASTS.   When God made women, He intended that they should have babies. A tiny baby has no way of feeding himself and would die without milk. God arranged it so that mothers could give their babies the food they need to live, and this milk comes from the mothers' breasts. Mothers need bigger breasts than fathers do, so that they can store the milk until their babies take it.

Many years ago, all babies were fed breast milk. Then some doctors found a way to make formulas like mothers' milk and to put it into bottles which babies could suck from. This milk is very good, but mothers' own milk usually is still best.

BREECH BABY. The usual way for a baby to be born is head first. But sometimes his buttocks or his feet are the first to come from the mother. Someone born this way is called a breech baby.

CAESAREAN SECTION. This is an operation that is done in special cases when the baby cannot be born in the usual way. This may be because the baby is too large or the mother's organs are not large enough.

A surgeon makes an incision in the abdomen and takes the baby out. The operation is named after Julius Caesar, who is supposed to have been born in that way. This today is a safe operation. A mother can safely have a number of babies by this method.

CALENDAR METHOD. See *Family Limitation.*

CELIBACY. This is a term frequently applied to the life of unmarried people. "Unmarried" is what the word means and suggests that the celibate by choice or circumstance does not give himself to sexual activity with a member of the opposite sex.

Priests, nuns and brothers take a vow of celibacy, which means that they promise God to give themselves completely to His service and never to marry. By the nature of God's laws, a life of celibacy—whether it is led by a religious or by a single person in the world—should mean complete abstinence from sex.

CERVIX. This is the opening of the uterus. It is about one inch long and is known as the neck of the womb. When a baby is being born, the cervix opens up to let it move from the uterus to the vagina.

CERVIX EXAMINATION METHOD. See *Family Limitation.*

CHASTITY. There is a great deal of misunderstanding about

this. Some people think chastity is only for certain people, like priests and nuns. Actually, chastity is for everybody, whether they're married or single, fourteen or fifty.

Chastity means using sex in the way God wants it to be used. Of course, the way God wants you to use sex depends upon your state in life.

God intended sex only for married people. The reason is that sexual intercourse is the means by which human life is begun, and babies can be cared for best if they have a mother and father living together as a family. Every unmarried person must avoid any of the acts of sex. And a married person must avoid such acts except with his partner. He also must not use sex in any way which violates God's law.

Sometimes the virtue of chastity requires that husbands and wives engage in the acts of marriage, because their marriage is helped by such love. There are other times when they ought to refrain from sexual activity. For example, a husband would have to control his impulses when his wife was sick or when he was away from home. A wife would have to practice chastity when it was not possible to have intercourse with her husband.

If you realize now that you must control your sex impulses and use sex only in specified ways, you'll be training yourself in chastity for life. Bringing your sexual powers under control now is the best possible training for the proper use of sex in marriage, or as a single person if that is your life.

CHILDBIRTH DANGERS. Before the twentieth century, it was fairly dangerous for a woman to give birth. The death rate for both mothers and babies was quite high. Now the situation is very different. A woman who goes to the doctor at the start of her pregnancy and who does what he tells her has an almost perfect chance of coming through in good health. For every 2,500 births, only one mother now loses her life, and that usually is a person who did not bother to go to a doctor or refused to follow his advice during her pregnancy.

A doctor encourages a pregnant woman to make regular visits so that he can keep a close check on her physical condition—her weight, blood pressure, and so on. He can tell whether the baby is growing normally. If anything is out of order, he can give the mother medicine to correct the condition and can also plan to take special precautions when the baby is delivered.

CIRCUMCISION. As the Bible tells us, just after Our Lord was born He was taken to be circumcised.

Circumcision was a very important religious ceremony of the ancient Jews, and it is still very important to orthodox Jewish people. It is a procedure by which the top skin of the penis is cut so that the head of the penis always stays uncovered. It is thought to be important to do this from a sanitary point of view. If dirt and discharges from the penis stay under the skin, they can cause serious disease later. When a boy is circumcised, it is easy to keep his penis clean. Most boys born in hospitals are circumcised.

A boy should be careful to keep that part of his body clean. When he takes a bath or shower, he should spread back the skin from around his penis, so that he can thoroughly clean the part that generally remains covered.

CLITORIS. This is a woman's organ immediately inside the opening of the vagina. It is similar in location and shape to the penis of the male, but is much smaller. This is the source of much of a woman's sexual pleasure.

CLOTHING. We wear clothing for two reasons. We need

it to protect our bodies from the cold, rain, snow, and from the heat and sun—we'd get terribly sunburned without it. When we walk in the street, we need shoes, because our feet would be hurt if we stubbed our toes or happened to step on broken glass, a sharp stone, a nail, or something else that might cut our skin.

The second reason we wear clothing is to keep the private parts of our bodies covered. These are the sex organs, which we do not show to everyone. That is why, even when you go to the beach and people are trying to get a suntan on their bodies, they all must wear bathing suits to keep from showing some parts of their bodies.

COITUS.   Another name for the act of intercourse.

COMPANIONS.   Years ago, there was a popular expression, "Tell me your friends and I'll tell you what you are." Even longer than that, people have been saying that "birds of a feather flock together." What was true hundreds of years ago is also true today. The kind of person you are is generally shown by the kind of person you associate with.

There's a great deal of truth to what is said about companions, as you can probably see for yourself. In your own school, probably certain groups of girls and boys always go around together, and you always see them together. Some of these groups may be on the wild side, some may be considered a little too tame, some may be more interested in sports than anything else, and some may be more interested in dates. Some may be the best students and others may generally give their teachers a hard time. Whatever they are, you know from your own experience that boys and girls with the same interests and backgrounds tend to pal around together.

Once you get in with a group, you know perfectly well you want to be one of them, and to do the same things they do. That's natural and understandable, and there's nothing wrong with it. But what you should make sure of is that the things this group wants to do are things that you yourself would never be ashamed of doing.

Most things that youngsters do are pretty harmless. But sometimes some of them get out of line, and into plenty of trouble. Sometimes, they can't even see this danger themselves. They're like people on a raft, traveling downstream on a river. They seem to be perfectly safe because the river's flowing at a slow pace. Right now, they could steer the raft over to the side of the river and step onto safe ground. They don't know that around the bend the river gets narrow and turns into rapids. If they stay on that raft all the way, they're going to be caught in a raging current before they know it. Somebody who's been over the area and knows the river could warn them that before long they would be in trouble. If they were smart they would take his advice. They might be inclined to laugh at the warning right now though, because everything seems good and safe.

Bad companions are like people together on a raft heading for a dangerous falls. They may feel safe now, but before long they'll be in serious danger. And it will be almost impossible to get off safely once the raft is carried around the bend and the current speeds up.

The point is to travel on a raft that's heading in the right direction, and that people who've been over the course assure you is the safe way to travel. And you'll do that by choosing companions who are heading in the right direction. They'll help you a great deal because they'll help you develop interests that will keep you morally safe and enhance your future, not endanger it.

CONCEPTION. This word describes what happens when the sperm from the male unites with the egg of the female. The moment this union takes place is a moment of creation and according to God's plan a new life begins. Right then God gives the new life a soul. So the tiny cell which will grow into a baby in about nine months is a precious being in the eyes of God, and has as much right to live as any human being.

CONFESSION. For the Catholic, Confession is to the soul what a good bath with soap and water is to the body. It cleanses the soul of sin and provides the grace we all need to amend our lives, and to keep from making the same mistakes over again.

Never be afraid or ashamed to go to Confession. The priest is there to listen sympathetically to your problems and to help you try to lead a better life. Don't think you'll shock him. He's heard it all before.

If you examine your conscience regularly and go to Confession often, you will find that the graces of the Sacraments will help you obey the Commandments much better than it is possible to do without them. By receiving the Sacrament of Penance and going to Holy Communion often, you'll be putting yourself in the best possible spiritual condition to handle all the temptations that are bound to come your way.

CONSUMMATION. A marriage isn't fully complete until the husband and wife unite in an act of coitus or intercourse. When this takes place, the marriage is said to have been consummated.

CONTRACEPTION. There is probably no more serious talk that a parent can have with an about-to-be-married son or daughter than about contraception.

Let me make clear what I am talking about. When I use this word I am not speaking of the size of your family-to-be or spacing your children. Having or not having children is a different question. Contraception literally means "against conception" and refers to the prevention of creating new life by means which are artificial, mechanical or chemical.

You will find that many people outside the Church act as if the end justifies the means, that deciding not to have children means permission to use any method which would keep the male sperm from uniting with the female ovum or which would destroy either cell at some time during the procreative process.

The Catholic knows otherwise. He knows that how something is done is just as important to good moral living as why it is done. This is what the Ten Commandments are all about. We must be careful of the kinds of things we do. No matter how completely we understand the pressures on a captured soldier, we would hardly look with favor on a man who betrayed his country, even to save himself some inconvenience or sacrifice.

And so it is with birth regulation. Regardless of the situation, the Catholic couple must never use a contraceptive in their love-making. They must always preserve the sanctity of their marriage bed.

God made man male and female. But that does not mean that He sent them off to work out their purposes without any reference to Him. He wants husbands and wives to love each other but wants that love always consecrated to Him, too, and expressed in the right way.

A man eats to satisfy his hunger. He eats not for the sake of eating but to live, even when he does not think of this or when his food is not actually nourishing. Likewise, man and woman in marriage ordain themselves by intercourse to parenthood, even when they are not thinking of a child, or when the conception of a child is in fact impossible.

There are only two ways really to control one's family size: by regulating sexual intercourse, or by frustrating the natural result of sexual intercourse. This latter is contrary to God's law for several reasons: one, because it excludes God completely from marriage; two, because by contraception man changes substantially the very nature of the marriage act, something he has no right to do.

Artificial birth control is an evil deed by its very nature. Like murder, blasphemy, adultery, no excuse can permit its use. And when practiced, the offense against God is a mortal sin because the interference with nature is serious. And one must remember that we deal here not with Church law but with God's law, which binds all men, Catholics and non-Catholics alike.

CONTRACEPTIVES. These are artificial devices, sometimes mechanical or rubber, sometimes chemical, used to prevent the conception of a baby or to destroy the tiny fertilized egg which is the first stage in a baby's life.

COPULATION. The union of male and female bodies in intercourse.

CURETTAGE. A minor operation occasionally performed on the mother after the baby is born. Usually all of the special lining of the uterus during pregnancy, the placenta, comes out of the body just after the birth. If some remains, the doctor performs a dilation and curettage, i.e., an enlarging and scraping of the womb to make sure no afterbirth remains there.

DANCING. As you've probably discovered by now, many things in life are perfectly fine if done the right way, but completely wrong if done the wrong way. For example, if you drive a car at forty miles an hour where the speed limit is fifty, you're obeying the law and driving safely as well, and your chances of reaching your destination without an accident are very high. But if you take advantage of a good thing and zoom along at eighty, you're misusing your car and may wind up with at least a speeding ticket and maybe a broken neck as well. So you see, it's often not things themselves that are wrong, but the way we use them.

It's that way with dancing. People have always enjoyed dancing. It's a perfectly wholesome thing to do, and very natural. When you hear a catchy tune, your natural impulse is to tap your feet in time with the music. If you do this with somebody you like, it's doubly enjoyable.

Not only that, but it's good exercise as well. Take a close look sometime at professionals who've spent their lives on the dance floor. Chances are they look a great deal younger than you'd ever expect them to be. All that exercise is good for the health. Dancing's also good for people who may be worried about their school work, marks, popularity, friends or anything else. It's hard to worry or think of anything unpleasant while you're keeping time with music.

Probably the one way to turn dancing from something good to something bad is to put too much sex into it. This generally happens when the dancers seem to be concentrating more on how close they can keep their bodies, than on keeping in step with the music. Of course, no boy should use dancing to bring his body into such close contact with a girl that it causes sexual thoughts. And no girl should allow it. If necessary, the girl should push a boy away if he tries to get too close. If that doesn't work, she should walk off the dance floor and wait for another partner.

DOUCHE. A washing out of the vagina with a syringe to keep it clean and free of odor.

There's nothing wrong with taking a douche for the purpose of cleanliness. However, most doctors don't think it is necessary, as a general rule. They say that ordinary washing when you take a bath or a shower is enough to keep the vagina clean and free of odor.

A douche is sometimes used as a contraceptive, and if it's used in this way it's sinful. To destroy sperm which has been placed in the vagina in intercourse is to interfere with the natural consequences of married love and as such is contrary to the very nature of the marriage act.

DREAMS. After a boy or girl has acquired the physical powers of an adult, he or she may start to have dreams with a strong sexual content.

For girls: Often a girl may dream of some great romantic love, in which a handsome knight swoops down and sweeps her off her feet. Sometimes she may even dream that she's engaging in intimate relations with him, and may find the dream very pleasurable. Since you're not responsible for your dreams, you needn't feel that there's any guilt attached to them. When you wake up, try to realize that what happened was really in a dream world and in no way resembles the way you should behave in real life. Just turn your mind to other matters and forget it.

For boys: Boys sometimes dream that they are engaging in sexual practices with other people. They may even have an orgasm and ejaculate semen. This ejaculation is nature's way of allowing you to dispose of your seed and to release your tension without sin.

You have no control over your dreams, and of course aren't held responsible when this happens in dreams. But you should avoid taking conscious pleasure from such dreams. The key word is "conscious." If you wake up in the middle of the dream, you shouldn't do anything consciously to continue it, or do anything consciously to stop it. And it would be wrong if you deliberately decided to continue the sensations you had or dwelled on them in your conscious mind. Sometimes, there may be a strong temptation to do this. Try to think of other matters, and get back to sleep.

These dreams that boys have are known as nocturnal

emissions, nocturnal pollutions, or wet dreams. A teen-ager may have one or two a week. It's nothing to worry about if you have more or less than this number. The important thing to remember is that wet dreams are natural and not sinful as long as you don't do anything to encourage them.

DRINKING. Once you are old enough, there's nothing wrong with drinking in moderation, at the right time and in the right place. Our Lord Himself drank wine, and He showed what he thought of it by the first miracle He ever performed, at the marriage feast at Cana, when He turned water into wine.

But like many other things that are all right in their place, drinking can be entirely wrong in other places. Of course, drinking so much that you lose control of yourself is always wrong.

Young people often don't realize the effects that alcohol can have on their will power and their understanding of what's right and wrong. The fact is that the more alcohol anybody drinks, the less able he is to control himself and his will power, and the more he finds himself doing things he'd never do in a million years if he were sober.

Another strange thing about alcohol is that it's hard to predict what its effects will be at any given time. A man may have two drinks today and feel perfectly fine, and feel no effect at all. If he has two drinks tomorrow on an empty stomach, or if he's upset or hasn't had a good night's sleep, he may find that he's unable to control himself nearly so well.

That's why drinking is especially dangerous on dates. A few glasses of beer may affect your ability to choose between what's right and wrong and your ability to resist temptation. When a boy and girl drink on dates they're playing with fire, because there's a danger that the drinks will get them to do things they wouldn't even consider doing if they were sober. Drinking keeps them from exercising their good sense to stay away from temptation, and it weakens their ability to handle a temptation if it comes their way.

Down through history, for thousands of years, the story has always been the same. More sins of impurity are probably committed when people are under the influence of alcohol than at any other time.

DYSMENORRHEA. This is a word doctors use to describe pain connected with menstruation. See *Menstrual Pain.*

EJACULATION. This is the forcible discharge of semen from the penis. Sometimes an ejaculation occurs at night and is involuntary. When it does, no sin is attached to it. But when a man (except one married, and then only during intercourse) does anything to produce this ejaculation, he commits sin.

EMBRYO. This word is used to describe a baby during the first three months of life in the mother's womb. The baby is generally called the fetus from the fourth month until it is ready to be delivered.

ENGAGEMENT. Many people think that when an engagement is announced it is time for the man and woman to accept congratulations all around. Engagement does mean marriage for most couples. But the idea that an engagement always leads to the altar is a mistake. When you become engaged you're usually just beginning to get really serious about marriage. If you get engaged, now is your time to find out whether your fiancé has the makings of a good lifelong partner. Now and only now will you be able to make a good judgment about your chances of a good life with this man or this woman.

This idea that engagement is the beginning of a search, and not the end of one, is important. You should never feel that once you become engaged, you have to go through with the ceremony no matter what. Millions of people would be better off if, during their engagement, they took a sharp look at the one they were thinking of marrying and realized that they couldn't live with that person the rest of their lives.

There are certain things an engaged person should watch for carefully. The most important is to make sure that the partner-to-be is capable of showing real love for another person. It may seem strange, but many people are unable to give real love. They are completely wrapped up in themselves. They try to get the best out of every situation that develops. They like to manipulate other people. They care very little about somebody else's feelings. If you are engaged to someone who insists on his or her own way all the time, and won't make sacrifices on your behalf, you can be sure your marriage will be headed for trouble.

Unselfishness, the willingness to make sacrifices for another person, is the one quality every successful marriage must have. Thousands of times in your married life—many times every day, in fact—a little consideration, thoughtfulness and interest in the other person's welfare will make the difference between a good marriage and one that causes pain and heartaches.

Whether people are selfish or unselfish often shows up in the way they look upon sex during the engagement period. Some people think that because they're engaged, they're entitled to all sorts of special privileges. That's completely false, because as you know the dividing line between what's permitted and what isn't is altered only by marriage, not by engagement. There's always a chance that an engaged couple will never marry—and the chances that they won't marry are greater if they have intercourse before marriage. And even if they do marry, marriage will call for control in scores of areas, control which should be in evidence during engagement.

Engagement should be a sacred time, a time when you're getting ready to receive a great Sacrament and take perhaps the most important step in your life. It is a time when you should think about spiritual matters and about all the responsibilities marriage involves, and should scrutinize closely the religious habits of your intended spouse, his desire for children, his congeniality, the married life of his parents, his work and social habits, his companions and countless other indications of stable personality.

ERECTION. The hard, rigid state of the penis when it is filled with blood. An erection can result from many factors. A boy may wake up with one after a long sleep. Or one may result when there is pressure on the bladder and a need to urinate, or when there is friction caused by tight clothing. An erection by itself is not wrong. But an erection can also result from stimulation and sexual excitement. It is wrong if a boy has one for that reason, and continues to dwell on sexual thoughts that cause the erection to continue.

"EVERYBODY DOES IT." All through your life, you will have to ask yourself the question, "What does God want me to do?" The answer you give has to be the thing you should do, because only in that way can you satisfy your conscience and live at peace with yourself.

There may be times when everybody does the right thing, the same as you do. For example, maybe everyone in your class or group habitually receives Communion at Sunday Mass. That's fine, and it's good for you to be with that group. But your own reason for receiving the Sacrament should be that by this means you honor God and draw nearer to Him. Whether everybody did it, or nobody did it, you should continue to do it, simply because it's the right thing to do.

Maybe at other times some people will do things that aren't right. Even if everybody did these things, it wouldn't make them right, for the simple reason that it's not what God wants you to do.

Suppose everybody decided all of a sudden that it was OK to steal and that if someone's back were turned, you could get away with his wallet or anything else that might be lying around. Now we know perfectly well that if everybody decided to steal, it would still be wrong for the simple reason that God told us so. If everybody decided it was all right to murder anybody who made them feel angry, and you could get away with killing as many people as you liked, that still wouldn't make it right, because you would still have to answer to the law of God, "Thou shalt not kill."

Of course, there's little chance that people will decide that murder, stealing or any other violations of the Ten Commandments are now perfectly suitable. The vast majority of people still believe in God and in His Commandments, and you'll find that if any Commandment is being broken, it's being broken by a small minority of the population.

It's nice to feel that everybody else thinks and acts the same as you do, but that's not the most important consideration. There are times in everybody's life when he has to stand up for what he believe to be right, even if there are very few people to support him. But when you stand up for your principles you're going to reap the greatest reward from God, because you're standing with the One Who is more important than any human being or any group of human beings. You're doing what God wants, and because of this, you can be sure that you'll lead a life which gives you a greater sense of satisfaction than those who go along with the crowd and then have to live with a guilty conscience all their lives.

FAMILY LIMITATION. When Catholics marry, they ought

to start out with the notion that they have a serious job ahead of them—to bear and rightly rear children. This means that they are not called to marriage merely to have a good time.

But being able to have children at any given time and being equipped at all times to take care of another child are different matters. Sometimes a husband and wife may have serious reasons for not wanting a child. When these reasons exist, they may limit the size of their family in a natural way.

These legitimate reasons why a couple might not want a child at a particular time are very broad. They can be economic, social, medical or eugenic.

As a practical matter, a couple might not want a child if they couldn't support him properly or give him the care and attention he needed, if the wife would be seriously ill or would risk her health, or if the couple thought their child would be physically or mentally defective in some way.

If a couple have a legitimate reason, they don't need anybody's permission to avoid having a baby. But they must make sure that both of them agree on what they're doing. The reason is that the natural way of avoiding birth requires the husband and wife to abstain from intercourse on days when the wife is fertile—that is, when she has an egg cell in a position where it could be fertilized by the male. This period of abstinence is always at least four days out of every month and might even be four or five days, depending upon how regular the wife's menstrual cycle is, and the method used to determine when she is fertile.

When they choose this method, the husband and wife must also be sure that other sins do not become part of their married life, for example, adultery.

Calendar Method. This is a natural means of practicing

family limitation which is based on the fact that most women menstruate at fairly regular intervals. For example, a woman may be able to predict that her menstrual cycle runs anywhere from twenty-seven to thirty days. By keeping records of when she menstruates, she can also predict approximately when she will ovulate, that is, when an egg cell will leave her ovary and move to the uterus. It is only around this time of ovulation that the egg cell can be fertilized and a baby can be conceived.

If she wishes to have a baby, she will have intercourse at that time of ovulation. If she doesn't wish to have a baby, she will avoid intercourse then.

Obvious-Ovulation Method. This is another way of determining when a woman is fertile, and when intercourse is likely to result in a baby. It can be used by comparatively few women. It is based on the fact that every time some women ovulate, they experience definite symptoms, like cramps, clots of blood, headaches, diarrhea or a sense of pressure on the abdomen.

Since the only time a woman can become pregnant is either just before, during or just after ovulation, if she knows from these signs that she's ovulating, she'll know exactly when intercourse would result in a baby. So this knowledge tells her when to have sexual relations with her husband if they want a baby, or when to avoid relations if they do not want one.

Test-tape Method. This is another way of determining when a woman is entering the time when a baby might result from intercourse. Around ovulation time, there is an increase in the amount of glucose found in the vagina. The test-tape is a specially prepared paper which tells when there is more glucose than usual. When the woman puts it in her vagina, it turns a light blue a few days before ovulation and a dark blue at the exact time of ovulation.

There is no change in color when ovulation is not at hand. Doctors do not all agree that this is a reliable method. It seems to work for some women but by no means all.

Body-Temperature Method. At the time of ovulation, there is also an increase of hormones in the woman's body, which causes an increase in her body temperature. If she takes her body temperature regularly and keeps careful records, she may be able to tell fairly accurately just when ovulation takes place, and, therefore, when conception is possible.

This method is generally considered the most reliable way for a wife to determine her fertile period. However, it is a little complicated, and it is necessary for her to get instructions from a competent doctor before she relies on it.

Cervix-Examination Method. This method is based on the fact that there's a distinct change in the mucous in the cervix around ovulation. The amount of this mucous increases just before ovulation, gets very heavy during ovulation, and also watery and a different color, and then changes to its original appearance after ovulation.

The woman who wants to use this method should go to a qualified doctor who will explain what the various changes mean. By examining her own cervix, she could then tell when she is fertile and when she is not able to begin a baby.

At some time you may legitimately wish to postpone pregnancy. Since to do this rightly you need some definite knowledge about the wife's ovulation pattern—her own, not just anybody's—an engaged girl might be wise to begin keeping records of her periods and to make observations of her own monthly indications. This knowledge will be useful in marriage.

FEARS OF SEXUAL INFERIORITY. Teen-age boys and girls may not like to admit, let alone talk about, some of their fears, particularly to their parents. If you have a problem and don't want to talk to parents about it, take it to some older person you trust—perhaps a parish priest or a teacher.

But in his own way, every adult has had fears of his own. When they were girls, many of today's mothers actually believed they would never be able to have a baby. Some men who are now husbands spent several unhappy years during their late teens thinking that no girl would ever want to marry them.

They were probably more afraid of the unknown than anything else. Right now, you're probably a chip off the old block. All the odds are that you are perfectly normal and the worst thing that can happen is for you to develop some secret fear about which you do nothing but worry. It's always a bit terrifying to look ahead to a new and difficult experience.

If you have a real worry, don't let it fester. The smart thing to do is to get it out in the open. That's why we find our school nurses and family doctors so important. Use them.

FERTILE PERIOD.   The time during the menstrual cycle when a woman could become pregnant. Doctors generally believe that the fertile period lasts no longer than four days in each cycle.

FERTILIZATION.   This is what happens when a baby is conceived. The male sperm enters the egg of the mother and fertilizes it.

FORESKIN.   The part of the skin covering the head of the penis. This is the skin that is cut off in circumcision.

FORNICATION.   This is the sin committed by an unmarried person who has sexual intercourse.

FRIGIDITY.   This word describes the condition of a man or woman who derives no pleasure from the sexual act. The cause is almost always psychological—at least so the doctors say. A common cause is the mistaken idea that even when sex is engaged in by a husband and wife for the purpose of having babies, it's somehow dirty and indecent. Another cause is that an unwanted pregnancy will result. Usually these frigid people don't realize it, but they're saying in effect that God made a mistake when He created sex, and that no "decent" person should engage in it. Of course, they're all wrong.

GENITALS. These are the principal sexual organs—the penis of the male, the clitoris and vagina of the female.

GLANS. The head of the penis or clitoris.

GONORRHEA. A venereal disease usually contracted as a result of sexual intercourse. See *Venereal Disease*.

GOING STEADY. A young man and woman usually go through several distinct stages before they marry. The first stage is ordinary dating. They may go out just once to some special affair, like a school basketball game, a dance or a special party. They realize that the date is for one time only. Maybe the boy will ask the girl to another event some time later, or maybe not. It's all very informal.

Next comes the stage of going steady, when the boy and girl see a great deal of each other alone, without going to dances or on dates with other people. He's her boy friend and she's his girl friend. If a dance, party or other event is planned, they take it for granted that they'll go with each other.

Next comes engagement. This is the stage that directly follows their going steady. Of course, when a couple become engaged, they usually set a date for the wedding. They're rapidly approaching the time when they'll be husband and wife. So you can see that going steady is an important preliminary step to getting married.

Nobody has set down a rule that this is how it should be. Nobody has to. It's the natural way things work out. So when any two persons begin going steady, there's a strong chance that they'll get married. That's why it's strange to see sophomores and juniors and even freshmen in high school restricting all their social activities to one person of the other sex. It's strange because the average high-schooler won't be ready to marry for four or five years at the earliest.

There's been found to be a definite relationship between the ages when a girl and boy first go steady and when they marry. Those who go steady at twelve or thirteen, for example, are more likely to get married when they're seventeen or eighteen than those who hold off until they're at least in their senior year in high school.

Now there's nothing morally wrong with getting married at seventeen or eighteen, of course, but when you consider all the responsibilities a married person has, you'll probably agree that the average person of that age takes on too great a burden if he marries. When a boy and girl decide to marry, they must be willing to become parents and take on the responsibilities of caring for their children. They have to be ready to make a great number of sacrifices, to do without many things they might want, to give their children the food, clothing, medical care and other things they need. They have to be ready to give up good times they might otherwise have and stay home with their youngsters.

Another bad thing about going steady is that it would keep you from getting to know more about the opposite sex generally and from being able to study what characteristics you'd like in a partner. Nobody would shop for a house, a car, or even a suit or dress that way. If you were buying a car, you'd want to see the dozens of different models, look at their motors, see how they were designed, and so on. When you're shopping for something far more important—a person you're going to live with all your life

—it makes sense to be at least as particular. You should want to get to know other persons who might be your marriage partner.

You may think your parents and teachers are "old fogies" when they tell you that it's unwise to go steady until you're ready to marry. But they have had far greater experience than you. They have seen the whole picture and know that many of the problems of married people result from their going steady too young.

When two persons go steady for a long time, there's also a danger that they'll get into habits of heavy necking, petting and even intercourse. Sometimes those things just grow. One thing leads to another and before they know it, they're committing serious sin.

One more thing. It stands to reason that if you want a good place in society when you're older, you won't want to marry so young because it may mean you'll have to give up all your chances of going to college or even, in some cases, of finishing high school. A person without at least a high-school education doesn't have much of a chance of getting a good job, and for any important job he needs a college education. It's very hard for a boy of eighteen or nineteen with a wife and family to support to spare the expense and time involved in getting a college education. So he and his family are stuck in a rut for life, because he couldn't wait a few years to marry, and he couldn't wait a few years to marry because he started going steady when he was too young.

So, it all adds up to the advice that nobody should begin to go steady until he is near the end of his education and ready to marry. No matter how you look at it, going steady is just a few steps removed from getting married, and it's foolish to start taking these important steps toward marriage until you're ready for the final step.

GROWING UP. Becoming an adolescent means a great deal
more than just adding another birthday or two. It
means that you're going to experience sharp but gradual
changes in your body, and that your attitudes and
ideas about things also will change. You're entering an
in-between stage—the stage between being a child and
being an adult.

The changes of adolescence are controlled by hormones,
which transform you from a child into an adult who could
become a mother or father. Hormones are chemical sub-
stances produced by the glands and carried by the blood to
the various parts of the body. By the marvelous process of
growth that God designed, these hormones start to work
as though on a pre-arranged signal around the time you
become a teen-ager. They're responsible for the physical
changes that turn a boy into a man and a girl into a woman.

The main gland that controls growth is the pituitary
gland, which is situated beneath your brain. It produces
several different kinds of hormones, which control your
rate of growth, the shape of your body, and other factors.

With all these physical changes going on in your body,
you're bound to feel other effects. Sometimes the hormones
pour into your bloodstream in uneven quantities, and they
may affect how you think and act at certain times. Sometimes you'll feel depressed for no reason you can put your
finger on, and sometimes you may feel like you're on top
of the world. Sometimes you'll feel as though you don't
have a worry in the world, and at other times you'll feel as
though you're carrying the whole world's share of them.
At times you'll probably think your parents don't understand you, and maybe once in a while you'll think they
understand you too well.

The point is that if you realize that hormones may affect

your mental attitudes at times, you won't get quite so depressed as you might get otherwise, because you have the knowledge that these moods will probably go away as quickly as they came. After sixteen or so, the hormones slow down quite a bit and you'll find you can lead a more peaceful existence with yourself.

One big problem teen-agers have with their parents arises when the teen-agers think that because they've grown up so much physically, they're all ready to take care of themselves. You realize, of course, that you still have a long way to go, and that it's necessary for your parents to keep looking after you to make sure you don't make any serious mistakes with your life.

It's important for you as an adolescent to realize that with every increase in your development and your abilities to do things for yourself, there's also a duty to use your new power in the right way. Having the power of sexual passion does not mean that you can use it any way you please. You must use it in the way God requires. And that means you must not use this power of passion until you're married and prepared to take care of any children who might be born as a result of it.

Changes in girls. Hormones change the appearance of a girl quite a bit after about the age of eleven to fourteen. Until then, if you cut a girl's hair and dressed her in a boy's slacks and shirt, it might be hard to tell that she was really a girl. Young boys and girls have pretty much the same body shapes.

But starting about the age of eleven in some girls and later in others, these hormones cause a number of developments designed to enable them to become mothers. They cause the hips to round out so a woman can give birth to a baby. They make the breasts rounder and fuller, so the mother can breast-feed her new baby. They cause the growth of the organs which are used to conceive a baby and to give the baby a home inside the mother's body.

Other changes also can be expected. You will find that hair begins to grow thicker under your arms, on your legs and around your genitals, or sex organs. You'll also notice changes in your voice. It will become fuller and richer—more melodious. With these changes, there'll be little chance that you could still be mistaken for a boy.

The most important change is menstruation. When you menstruate, you discharge a quantity of blood every twenty-eight days or so. This is perfectly natural and normal and is no cause for alarm. It happens to every female. It's one stage in the plan God devised so that a woman could take care of a baby inside her body if one were started.

When a little girl is born, God has already given her all the organs she'll need to become a wife and mother. Every healthy girl has two tiny ovaries in her lower abdomen. These are shaped like almonds, and through the tremendous beauty of God's plan, they contain countless tiny egg cells from which a baby could grow.

Of course, in a baby girl, these ovaries are only a tiny part of what they will be when she grows up, just as your fingers and toes as a baby were very small compared to what they are now.

The ovaries stay small during childhood. But when a girl is about to become a young woman, the ovaries also grow. The ovaries play an important part in a woman's life. Every month or so, one of the two ovaries discharges a tiny egg cell in a process known as ovulation. As a rule, this ovulation takes place about once every twenty-eight or thirty days. A girl begins to ovulate around the ages of twelve to fourteen and continues to do so on this regular

basis until she's about forty-five. Doctors aren't completely
sure exactly how the ovaries work in every case, but generally speaking, one ovary releases an egg one time and the
other ovary releases an egg the next time, twenty-eight or
thirty days later.

One of these egg cells is no bigger than the dot you could
make with a pencil. But God has arranged it so that it contains all of the mother's characteristics that a baby might
inherit—maybe the color of her skin and hair, and so on.
After it leaves the ovary this egg moves into a long, narrow
tube known as the Fallopian tube, and then into the uterus,
or womb.

God has seen to it that a baby cannot be born unless
there is a man to be the father—somebody who could take
care of the mother and the baby. That's why He created
the idea of marriage, and that's why He devised it so that
the egg from the mother's ovary cannot produce a baby
all by itself. For a baby to be born, the egg cell must
first be united with a seed from the father's body.

Every month there's a chance that a baby can be conceived. An egg is discharged whether the female is married
or not. Just in case the egg will be united with the male
seed, it's logical that the woman's body should be ready so
that she could carry, feed and nourish a growing baby if
one were conceived.

As you may know, the uterus, or womb, is the part of a
woman's body God designed as the resting place of the
baby for the nine months he's developing in his mother's
body. In order to be ready if a baby is going to begin to
grow in the woman's body, the uterus has a lining which
would surround the fertilized cell and would nourish it for
nine months. Of course, a young girl is not going to become a mother. So something must happen to the egg cell
which hasn't been fertilized and to the lining of the uterus

which hasn't been used. If the egg hasn't been fertilized, it disintegrates in the body and disappears. The lining of the uterus, the endometrium, also separates from it, and with a supply of blood which has been built up, it passes through the body. When this blood is discharged, menstruation begins. Menstruation occurs about fourteen days after the egg leaves the ovary.

A girl's first menstruation is a sign that she's beginning to be physically equipped to have a baby. But her body must continue to grow for quite a while before she could safely have a full-grown baby. And, of course, a girl of fourteen or so isn't old or responsible enough to take on the lifelong job of caring for a child. At the very youngest, only a girl in her late teens is mature enough to become a mother.

Most girls don't menstruate regularly for a year or so. At the beginning, two months or even more may elapse between menstrual periods. Gradually the periods draw closer together. After a few years, they come with a great deal of regularity, within a difference of a few days or so every time. Most women don't have exact cycles. You might have one period of twenty-eight days, then one of twenty-seven days, then one of thirty days. Generally a girl can predict within two or three days when her period will begin.

It's not important now for you to pinpoint the exact date anyway. Years ago, girls thought they just had to shut themselves up during menstruation and considered themselves sick. They wouldn't go swimming or bathing or engage in any athletics or go dancing. We now know that a girl can carry on as usual during this period. It's even possible to go swimming, although a few precautions should be observed. According to the American Medical Association, the only time a girl may have to cut down is on the first day or so. It's generally all right to swim even then, as long as you avoid violent exercise and keep from getting overtired or chilled, if the water is too cold. Of course for sanitary reasons, you shouldn't want to swim in a pool or other tiny area where you might cause hygienic problems.

If you think you should curtail your activities at this time, you shouldn't feel any embarrassment about it. Just remember that menstruation is natural for every girl. If someone invites you to do something you don't think you should do, you can just say that you can't do it for a day or so. You don't have to give any further explanation unless you want to.

You might sometimes feel constipated during menstruation. Sometimes there's a certain amount of pressure exerted on the lower bowels. If this happens, just treat the constipation the same as you would at any other time. Drink plenty of liquids, like water or milk, or even soft drinks, and eat a lot of raw fruits and vegetables which will help keep your bowels open.

It's important to bathe often and keep yourself free from body odors at this time. Try to take a shower or give yourself a sponge bath every day. It's generally not wise to take a regular bath, because you want to reduce the danger of infection to the minimum. But don't think that you can get away from a sponge bath or shower by using a deodorant or perfume. You may find that you have to use too much of it, and its odor may be more offensive than the one you're trying to cover.

Naturally, you'll have to wear sanitary napkins that will absorb the discharge and keep it from spotting or spoiling your clothing. These napkins come in different sizes and can be held in place with sanitary belts.

Some people use tampons. These are smaller pads, made to fit inside the vagina. They contain less cotton than the larger pads worn outside, so they may have to be changed more often. Anyway, it's a good idea to change pads at least twice a day, and probably several times the first day of menstruation. See also *Menstrual Cycle, Menstrual Pain.*

Changes in boys. You can expect hormones to start doing their work from the age of twelve onward. The first big sign that they're on the job is that they cause you to grow faster than you've grown before. Until now, you probably grew no more than five or six inches in your best year. Now you may gain eight, ten, even a dozen inches. You'll find that a pair of pants you bought new a few months before now may not even reach your ankles.

The next change is in your voice. Instead of being pitched high, it will move down a couple of notches. Sometimes the change may take a while. You may start talking in a low-pitched voice and suddenly discover that your voice has cracked and you're now talking at a higher pitch. There's nothing unusual about this. The only thing is that when your voice is changing, you should try not to do too much yelling or screaming. Too much of this might damage your larynx.

Another important change is that hair will begin to grow on your face and chest and around your penis. Sometimes boys also have a great deal of hair on their arms and legs. How much hair you have has nothing to do with how strong you are or how much of a man you are. The amount of hair people have depends to a large extent on their background. Dark-haired people generally have more hair than light ones. So if you don't have much hair on your face or chest, don't worry about it. As a matter of fact, you'll probably be glad of it later because you won't have to shave as often as some people with thick growths who need to shave twice a day.

The biggest and most important change of all is in the size of your penis and testicles. They grow to make it possible for you to engage in the act of sex—the act which will enable you to become a father.

In addition to growing, the penis develops the ability to ejaculate semen. This is a thick liquid substance containing sperm. When sperm fertilizes an egg cell in a woman's body, a baby is conceived. In this way, God gives you the gift of sharing with Him in the act of creation—creating a new human life. As you can see, that's a sacred responsibility and that's why your power to perform the sex act must be guarded very carefully.

Some boys think the size of their penis is also a sign of how much manhood they have. It is no such thing. Size has nothing to do with a person's ability to become a father.

Sometimes you may wake up to find you've discharged in your sleep and that you've wet your pajamas or bed with it. That is a way God has provided to dispose of extra semen your body has produced. You may even have sexy dreams while this ejaculation is going on. There's nothing sinful about this as long as you didn't deliberately cause it. If you wake up and discover that this is going on, you shouldn't do anything to stop it or keep it going. Just let nature take its course and try to go back to sleep.

This power of passion which God gives you at adolescence is the power to bring a new life into the world, a little baby made in God's Image and Likeness and with a soul all his own. It's such a great power that God gives you that it should be guarded with the greatest care. If you had a precious diamond, you'd put it in a safe place under lock and key, to make sure it wouldn't be stolen from you. You should do the same with the power of your sex. Don't let it be dragged through the mud as though it were worthless.

HOMOSEXUALS. A homosexual is a person, usually a man, who has sexual relations with members of his own sex.

There are also women homosexuals called lesbians.

Homosexuality is a sickness. Psychotherapists and doctors don't seem to agree on the exact causes, and it's possible that several causes are involved. A homosexual usually doesn't want to be the way he is. He knows, of course, that when he has sexual relationships with other men he's doing something unnatural, and something contrary to the intentions God had when He made the sex organs. God made man for woman, and vice versa.

Older male homosexuals often try to get young boys to sin with them. Sometimes they become very friendly and offer the boys all kinds of gifts to try to win them over. Sometimes boys who sin in this way get into the habit and find that they can't live a normal life thereafter. For this reason, boys should be very careful about becoming friendly with strange men who are older than themselves.

But it's a mistake to think that every man who may act a little effeminate is a homosexual. Appearances are often deceiving. Some homosexuals are six-footers who look like real he-men. On the other hand, a boy or man with so-called effeminate interests in such things as art and music may be more masculine than the average.

The only test of a homosexual is whether or not he commits sexual perversions. A person who may seem effeminate but who leads a pure life should not be condemned. On the other hand, there's no reason why those who flaunt their unconventionality and make no secret that they practice perversion should be treated tolerantly.

HYMEN.   This is a thin membrane at the opening to the vagina. It's generally not painful if it's broken but breaking it usually causes bleeding.

In former times, it was generally thought that an intact hymen was a sign that a girl was still a virgin, because if intercourse took place, the hymen would have broken.

Therefore, some people looked for signs of blood after the wedding night. If it wasn't found, they suspected the bride of having had premarital intercourse.

We now know that the hymen may be broken in many different innocent ways—by a girl engaged in athletics, for example, or by some kind of accident. So it's both wrong and foolish to say that just because the hymen has been broken, a girl is no longer a virgin.

ILLEGITIMACY. Babies born to unmarried mothers are said to be illegitimate. It is an unfair and cruel thing to do, but many people put a stigma on these babies, who are also described as being born out of wedlock. Another word for such a baby used in former days was bastard. The fact that this is now considered a dirty word shows how people look on the child of an unmarried mother.

Even if an illegitimate baby were not looked down upon, there would still be many powerful reasons for unmarried people to think a few dozen times before they engage in intercourse.

But when you think of all that is involved, not only in having a baby but in taking care of it, you'll realize the terrible risk. After intercourse, it takes roughly nine months for the baby to develop inside the mother's body—a time when the mother would have to take it easy, and would need somebody to take care of her and even provide for her. If she didn't have a husband to do this for her, she would have mighty tough going. She might even have to depend on charity from outsiders, or go to some charitable institution which would take care of her.

But that's just the beginning. When a baby is born, he's completely helpless and will be that way for years and years. A parent has to count on taking care of a child, feeding him, clothing him, seeing that he gets all kinds of doctor and dentist care for eighteen years at least, and if he goes to college, even longer than that. You can imagine what a job it would be for an unmarried mother to support herself and her baby and to give him all the love and attention he needs for that length of time.

Then there's the question of how a baby can grow up without a father's care. To grow up properly, both boys and girls need to be close to some man—if not their father, then somebody else. They need a clear picture in their minds of what a man is and how he acts, and what kind of a job he does in life. A boy needs a model so he can get an idea of how he himself is expected to act when he grows up. A girl needs a model too, so she can learn how to get along with men and what their natures are. In that way she'll be a better wife and mother when she grows up.

All in all, you can see it's a might heavy burden that an unmarried girl takes on herself when she has an illegitimate baby. It's important to remember where this whole thing begins. It starts by having intercourse outside of marriage.

You'll hear talk that you can surely avoid having a baby by using contraceptives. That just isn't true. More contraceptives are being used today than ever, and there are also more illegitimate babies. All kinds of statistics prove that contraceptives are no foolproof guarantee that a boy or girl can have their cake and eat it too. In fact, the chances of a contraceptive failing, or being used incorrectly, are so great that anybody who counts on their being completely safe, is completely wrong.

IMPOTENCE.   A person who's impotent is unable to perform the sexual act. The reasons may be physical or psychological. Since it's the man who takes the active part in the sex act, there's rarely any physical reason why a woman couldn't take part in it. Usually it's only men who are said to be impotent. Once in a while, a woman's vagina is so small that penetration is impossible. In this circumstance, she too would be called impotent.

Don't confuse impotence with sterility. A sterile person can perform the act but is not able to contribute a healthy sperm if he's a male, or an egg, if she's a woman. This sterile person cannot be a parent.

A person who's permanently impotent cannot marry validly. The reason is that a valid marriage requires that both persons must be able to engage in intercourse. See *Frigidity*.

INDUCED ABORTION. This term describes an act when the baby in the mother's womb is deliberately destroyed to keep him from being born.

Doctors sometimes use the word abortion to describe any death of the baby in the womb—even when the mother doesn't want her baby to die and does everything possible to keep him alive. When the baby dies without the mother's wanting it to die, it is known as spontaneous abortion, and also as miscarriage.

Of course, having a miscarriage or spontaneous abortion is not a sin, because the mother doesn't make it happen. An induced abortion, which she does cause to happen, is another matter. It's a very grave sin, so grave in fact that only a priest with special power can forgive this sin.

Induced abortion is a serious sin because it is the deliberate taking of an innocent human's life. It is against the Commandment, "Thou shalt not kill."

Some people seem to think it's all right to kill an innocent baby in his mother's womb, but that it's wrong to kill him after he has been born. They don't realize that if it is wrong to kill a baby the day he's born, it is just as wrong to kill him while he's still in his mother's body. He's a human being from the time God breathes a soul into him, and that happens when his life begins in his mother's body.

Some people say that it's all right to perform an abortion

of a baby if the mother's life is in danger. But the Church says it's wrong to take one person's life to save another one's, and that's what happens when this kind of abortion is performed. Besides, the question of saving the mother's life *or* the baby's is an old-fashioned one. Today both lives can usually be saved.

Another point to remember is that if a mother is seriously ill, doctors can give her any kind of treatment she needs to save her own life as long as they don't *deliberately* destroy her baby. If the baby dies as an accidental result of these treatments or operation, nobody has done anything wrong. The point is that the operation wasn't performed with the direct idea of harming the baby.

INTERCOURSE. This is the means God made to let a husband and wife show their love for each other and to start the life of a baby. God gives each man a penis, and in intercourse the man places his penis in his wife's body. Some of the husband's seed called sperm leaves the penis and if it is God's will it unites with an egg in the wife's body. In this way a baby's life is begun.

INTERRACIAL MARRIAGE. God made all mankind, and we are all his children, no matter what the color of our skins. Because every person is equal in God's sight, no one can say it's wrong for one person to marry another person who may be a member of a different race. In fact, it's completely wrong and un-Christian to look down on any other person because his color is different.

While there are no religious reasons why two persons of different races shouldn't marry, an interracial couple must make the same practical judgment that is expected of people with similar racial background: Will this union be a stable one? And so the interracial couple face the same difficulties as those who come from different religious, social, or cultural levels. In these cases love alone does not suffice, and obviously neither does it suffice for the interracial marriage.

KISSING. Probably for as long as anybody can remember, the question has been asked whether a girl should let herself be kissed on a date.

Before answering that, you have to realize that kissing on the lips is quite different from kissing on the cheeks, the way old friends do. There's a certain stimulation created by lip-kissing, because the lips are a sensitive part of the body.

The question to kiss or not to kiss depends to a certain extent on how long you've known the one involved and what he or she means to you. It's not wise to kiss anybody on the first or second date. The boy who tried to make a great deal over a kiss gives the impression that he's not really interested in the girl herself, and a girl who lets herself be kissed the first time out gives the impression that she's an easy mark. The boy with her may get the idea he should advance a few steps on the next date.

You may have heard about the comparison someone made between kissing and wine. He said a kiss on the lips is like a sip of wine. Maybe it won't do any harm. A prolonged kiss is like a glassful of wine. It might be enough to make someone lose his common sense. A long smooching session is like several glasses of wine, with the wine-drinker on the verge of being drunk. The persons who kiss too much may be in the same boat—on the verge of letting their passions get the better of them.

LABOR. This is the term given to the activity of a mother just before the baby is born. In labor, there is a coming together of the muscles of the uterus, where the baby has been for nine months. This forces the baby out of the uterus into the birth canal.

LESBIANISM. The immoral sexual relationship between two women.

LOVE. There's a great deal of confusion about the meaning of this word. It has only one real meaning. When you love somebody, you're interested in his welfare above all and you won't ever do anything to hurt him.

One of the best examples of human love is the kind a mother shows a child. She's willing to do everything necessary to help her child grow up strong and healthy, and to lead a good, decent life. That doesn't mean she gives him everything he wants, because there are many things children would like to have that parents know from experience won't be good for them. A mother wouldn't give her baby matches to play with just because the baby wanted them. She would realize that the baby might hurt himself, and for his own welfare she doesn't give him what he wants.

It's the same way with boys and girls. A boy who really loves a girl will be sincerely interested in her welfare. He won't want to do anything to cause her harm. When you look at love that way, you realize that the boy who's trying to persuade a girl to have intercourse with him is thinking entirely about himself, and not about her. If he really cared for her, he wouldn't want her to have such a sin on her conscience, or to feel the deep sense of shame that usually follows. And he certainly wouldn't want her to go through the agony that follows when she doesn't know whether she's pregnant or not and might have the shame of giving birth to a baby outside of wedlock.

Anybody who thinks sex outside marriage is love either doesn't know the meaning of the word love or he doesn't have the good sense to realize exactly what this so-called love can do to a girl. Sometimes a boy hands out a line that if a girl loves him, she'll give in. A girl who falls for this is a fool. The boy who uses it is actually proving that he doesn't really love her, and the girl could answer that a boy who loved her wouldn't be asking her to take on all the shame, heartaches and worry that follow intercourse outside of marriage.

Everybody would laugh at a boy who claimed he loved a girl and then asked her to join him in robbing a bank. They'd see clearly that if he really cared for her, he wouldn't ask her to commit a sin and also risk going to prison. The same situation exists when he asks her to join him in sinning against the Sixth Commandment. He's not thinking of her welfare but of his own satisfaction, and that kind of selfishness is the exact opposite of love.

MAGAZINES. See *Reading Matter.*

MARRIAGE PREPARATION. You can't make a good emotional or physical adjustment in marriage unless you understand just what makes a woman or a man. Despite everything that has been said these past few years, women and men are greatly different. They're different in how they look at the problems of life, in the things they consider important, in how they react to little incidents, in how they think and talk. Sometimes two women will engage in a conversation with their husbands present. The husbands will understand the words, but what the wives are really saying often will go over their heads.

For the groom. A man tends to say what he thinks in a direct way. A woman will say what she thinks, but often indirectly. The woman who hears her husband say something may wonder what he really means because she has been trained to search for hidden meanings. On the other hand, a husband who takes everything his wife says at face value, without trying to find out what she really means, will face a great number of misunderstandings in his married life.

You will have to understand your wife's nature. A woman tends to show her emotions to a greater extent than a man does and is also more intuitive. She may meet a friend of yours and tell you later she doesn't like him. If you try to pin her down, and to find what logical reason she has for her dislike, she doesn't have a black-and-white reason. She doesn't like his face, or there's just something about him she doesn't trust.

A woman also is less inclined to take the direct approach in getting what she wants. Unlike a man, who will probably come right out and say what he wants, a woman makes sure that she puts her husband in the right mood, by fixing a meal he likes, having his slippers ready when he comes home, telling him how attractive he looks, and so on. She likes to be treated in the same roundabout way.

You'll also make a mistake if you expect your wife to be crisp and decisive, and to make up her mind with a snap of the fingers, the way you may have learned to do at work. You'll have many annoyances when you go shopping if you expect her to act this way. The simple fact is that most women are slow, cautious, given to looking things over very carefully, a great deal less likely than a man to walk out of the shop with the first thing the sales clerk hands her.

All these characteristics have to be taken into consideration in trying to work out a good sexual adjustment with your wife. By nature, a man is sexually impulsive. He tends to want to rush through the act without adequate love-making. He also tends to separate the act of intercourse from other relationships between himself and his wife. But the husband who does this and doesn't make allowances for his wife's nature won't be a very satisfactory lover.

A wife wants the sexual act to be at least as much of a romantic and emotional experience as a physical one. She wants the soft-lights-and-music approach. She wants to know that you want her for herself, and not just because she has a woman's body. She wants you to be slow, gentle, reassuring and considerate.

It has been said that many marriages have been ruined on the wedding night because the husband proceeded to have intercourse without any real consideration of the fact that his wife was a partner. He was almost completely selfish in the way he went about it. But it just can't be that way. Your wife is entitled to pleasure and satisfaction and it's your job to prepare her emotionally and physically in a tender way so she can respond fully to your advances.

The act of intercourse can never be separated from the rest of your life. If you want a satisfactory sexual partner, you'll have to try to build up a feeling of mutual love and affection, and the only way this can be done is not during the act itself, but before it, after it, and all day long.

Never make sex a one-sided thing. It is an act of love. That means it's an act in which two people give of themselves unselfishly, their first concern being the well-being of their partner.

For the bride. One of the most important things a wife must learn is that a man is different from a woman in more ways than most people realize. He thinks differently, acts differently, tells what he thinks and what he wants in an entirely different way, reacts in a different way to everything from the cry of a baby to the ring of the telephone or the call of a bill collector. He is different in his attitudes toward marriage and life, toward home and work, even in what he thinks about love.

If you want a happy marriage, you'll have to understand your husband. Only by studying him at close hand can you really know what makes him tick. And only when you know what makes him tick will you be able to be the kind of wife he wants.

You'll make a big mistake if you expect your husband to be as enthusiastic as you are over a new bedroom set, or even to work up any great enthusiasm over saving for one. You'll have to learn to live with the fact that he's often a creature of impulse. Turn him loose with a shopping list and in most cases he'll probably take the first thing the sales clerk hands him.

He's usually not very emotional, and you may find that

it's hard to get him to express his deep inner feelings. Don't forget that men have been taught from childhood that it's not manly to cry or show other emotions as women do. As a result, it's sometimes hard for a woman to understand how they really feel deep down about certain things. But because your husband doesn't show it on the surface, don't think he doesn't have deep anxieties and a need to be appreciated.

Most people feel that they're not really understood, that nobody cares about their problems. The job a husband does of providing for the family and of worrying about bills for this, that and the other thing falls into a routine pattern. Sometimes his wife and children take it all for granted, and he may complain that they think he merely has to pluck what they want from a tree. He has his problems in his job —every man does—and it's a wise wife who encourages him to believe that she deeply appreciates him and understands his problems.

By nature, a man is usually quick on the trigger. He's a great deal more likely than a woman to blow up over some slight, real or imagined, than a woman is. He has to be handled with a great deal more care. You'll always get more out of him by using the soft feminine approach than you can by trying to stand up to him as a man would, slugging it out toe to toe. They say there isn't a woman born who can't get her way with her husband if she just uses patience and the right approach, and appeals to his desire to play the part of her protector and provider. If you appreciate your husband as a good, strong, competent individual, you'll find him doing almost anything you want.

These characteristics of the male show up in intercourse. He's impulsive and aggressive and can be stirred up sexually by things you wouldn't pay any attention to—by a whiff of perfume, a seductive look, even by a sexy picture. Once he starts to dwell on that subject, his desire builds quickly and he wants to have it brought to a conclusion. He's impulsive by nature and probably has to be encouraged to wait if necessary until his wife is ready. He wants to feel that he's a competent lover, and if you can make him feel that way by giving him the encouragement he needs, you'll be contributing to a good adjustment.

One of the best things you can do to help make a success of your marriage is to take a short course given at a Pre-Cana Conference or by the parish priest. Ask your fiancé to go with you where it will be possible to get answers to your intimate questions without embarrassment. If it's not possible to do this, ask the priest to recommend a good book on Catholic marriage. Such a book can give you a clear picture of all of the factors—spiritual, emotional and physical—that you should know about.

Sexual adjustment. It's a mistake to assume that sexual adjustment will come early in marriage. Any new husband and wife should expect a period of trial and error of years, or at least months, before they can achieve a reasonably good adjustment.

Although many books on this subject don't say so, a couple need a good spiritual and emotional adjustment before they can achieve true harmony in marriage. The act of sex means little unless it's an act of love—unless it embodies the unselfish desire of the husband and wife to help their partner achieve satisfaction.

Harmony in sex is impossible unless there's harmony in other relationships as well. Any discord over other matters will surely be reflected in the attitude of the husband and wife in this most important area.

So if you want a happy sexual life, you'll have to try to adjust yourself unselfishly to your partner in every other area. That's why it's always repeated that unselfishness is the greatest quality a person can bring into marriage, and that only when there's true love can there be good sexual relations.

Choosing a mate. The success of your marriage will naturally depend on the kind of person you choose as your partner. Good looks are only one consideration, and so is the feeling that you can have a good time with this person you'll spend your life with.

But a husband and wife need more than that in common if they're going to have a loving and harmonious life together. The expression "the honeymoon's over" tells the story. It means that marriage takes on an entirely different complexion when the husband and wife settle down to the day-in, day-out routine of living. Good looks and being able to have fun will mean a great deal less when you have a child to support, the monthly rent to pay, food to buy, and all the other responsibilities of living. Then other characteristics of your mate will become very important.

The first thing your partner should have is the same basic philosophy of living that you do. It doesn't matter so much if a spendthrift marries a spendthrift, because then neither one cares whether they've saved a nickel or not. They'd probably be happier than if one person wanted to spend everything and the other wanted to save it. But if you put together two persons who disagree about the basic problems of life and marriage, they'll find themselves at cross purposes half a dozen times every day of their lives.

That's one reason why mixed marriages so often come to a dead end. Everybody—Protestants, Jews, Catholics—agrees that it's much harder to make a go of a mixed marriage. They all know that a person brought up in one religion thinks entirely differently about some of the most important questions of life than does the person brought up in another religion. There's almost sure to be conflicts over where or whether the children should go to church on Sunday, whether it's right to practice birth control, what kind of food you should serve on Friday, whether divorce is right or not, and dozens of similar issues.

But a person is not a good bet as a marriage partner just because he happens to have the same religion. There are many other factors involved. Is he responsible? Will he do the job expected of him? A husband is expected to be head of the house, the provider. He's expected to take the responsibility of keeping a roof over his family's head and provide for the food, clothing and all its other needs. A wife is supposed to be the heart of the house, to take care of the children and the home. If one person isn't ready, willing or able to do the expected job, then the partner will have to take on the extra burden. That's unfair, and it's likely that the partner will resent it.

Is your prospective partner thoughtful and considerate? Dozens of times a day, an inconsiderate husband or wife can cause the other person to grit his teeth and resent what's happening. It's almost impossible to have a good marriage if one person is thoughtless, and the marriage is certainly heading for the rocks if both persons keep thinking of their own selves before anybody else. The person who's willing to be reasonable and to let you have your way once in a while is one of the best possible bets.

And steer away from the hot-blooded individual who hits the ceiling every time something goes a little bit wrong. You'd be surprised at the number of times a day something comes up between a husband and wife that can be handled in one of two ways. One of them can shrug and disregard what's been said or done—or the same person can decide to make a federal case of it. Marry a hothead and you'll feel as though you're spending your life walking on eggs, fearing you'll be shot if you crack one of them.

It's true that you marry the boy or girl—not the whole family. But it will pay to look the in-laws over, because that's the way your would-be mate may be twenty years from now. If the mother in particular seems too bossy, and your prospective mate is easily influenced by her opinion, the yellow caution light is blinking! Find out what your future parents-in-law think about marriage and sex, about the responsibilities of a husband and wife. Notice how they get along together, how courteously or discourteously they treat each other. You'll be getting a preview of how you'll be treated—and how you'll be expected to act. If you don't like this preview "in living color," you ought to think a few dozen times whether you'd be happy with the person who came out of such a family.

MASTURBATION. This is any handling of the genitals (the penis of the boy, the vulva of the girl) with the deliberate intention of deriving sexual pleasure.

Masturbation is always wrong, because it goes against the reasons God intended when he gave us these organs. He made men and women so they could unite their organs in marriage, mainly for the purpose of having children. Any other use of them for physical pleasure is a sin, because it's contrary to what He wants us to do.

It used to be believed that masturbation could cause all kinds of afflictions—blindness, deafness, skin disease, even insanity. That's not true.

But it's a sinful practice, and is not without psychological damage to the individual. It causes him to think of sex as a physical sensation for his private enjoyment, not as something sacred to be shared with a person you love. There's only a twisted kind of self-love involved in masturbation.

One thing everybody has to learn is how to control himself, and how to deal effectively with temptations of this kind. Everybody also has to learn how to recognize the thoughts and desires that make control of improper sexual fulfillment very difficult.

The most important way to keep this habit from taking hold of you is to make a resolution to receive the Sacraments regularly and to keep yourself in the state of grace. Go to Confession every week, and if possible, go to the same priest every time. Tell him you would like him to be your regular Confessor so that he can help you better to keep temptations under control. As you know, you should never be afraid to tell your deepest secrets to the priest in the Confessional. He is absolutely bound not to reveal what you say to anyone.

If you make it a habit to go to Confession and to receive Communion regularly, you'll find that the Eucharist serves as spiritual food. It strengthens your soul the way bread and meat strengthen your body. It's a good idea to think of the Communion rail as the spiritual banquet table.

Another habit to get into is to say your morning and evening prayers without fail. When you get up in the morning, ask God to keep you on the straight and narrow during the day, and to strengthen you so you won't violate any of His Commandments. If you keep God's other nine Commandments faithfully, you'll find it easier to observe the sixth one.

At night, always make an examination of your conscience. Try to figure out what you did wrong during the day. You know, there's an old saying that everybody makes mistakes but that the smart people figure out why they made them so they can prevent them in the future. Try to find out where you're weak and where your trouble lies. Before you go to sleep, ask God's forgiveness for anything you did that was out of line, and resolve to avoid those acts in the future.

There are two ways of looking at a sin or any other

mistake you make. The first way is to tell yourself that you're no good and never will be. The second way is to realize that you were wrong, and to feel guilty about your mistakes, but also to resolve to do better in the future. That determination to get off the floor and try to do better next time is what will help you to make success of your life, spiritually and every other way.

Go over in your mind under exactly what circumstances your temptations to commit sin arise. You'll find that there are certain patterns—that thoughts that enter your mind under some conditions wouldn't stand a chance at other times. By that I mean it's a thousand-to-one bet that no idea about violating the Sixth Commandment would occur to anybody who's getting ready to shoot a basket in the middle of a basketball game. The chances are much greater if he finds himself all alone, looking through a dirty magazine.

It's always a good idea to change the subject right away as soon as your mind starts dwelling on the pleasures of the flesh. The best way to change the subject is to start doing something active. Try to talk up a ball game, watch a good program on television, call up a friend, clean your room, wash your hair, or do something else you enjoy doing, that will keep you busy and take your mind off the temptation. Sometimes it's not easy, but you'll find that with practice it gets easier and easier to resist temptation, just as it gets harder to resist it if you give in to it every time.

MENOPAUSE.   Older ladies don't have babies because when they're in their middle forties or so their ovaries stop discharging eggs which could be fertilized by male sperm, and they stop menstruating. The beginning of menstruation is a sign that a girl can become a mother, and the end of menstruation—or menopause—is a sign that a woman no longer can become a mother.

MENSTRUAL CYCLE. This refers to the length of time from the beginning of one menstruation to the beginning of the next one. The normal or average cycle for many women runs about twenty-eight or twenty-nine days. But it may vary considerably.

MENSTRUAL PAIN. Menstruation is an entirely natural process, and most girls go through their menstrual periods without feeling any real pain. Sometimes there are mild pains like cramps or backaches just before menstruation begins or on the day blood begins to show. Severe pains are rare, and if these happen a doctor should be consulted.

A few days before menstruation, some girls feel as though they're bloated. They may also have feelings of depression. Everything seems to be wrong. A girl may be able to laugh off certain conditions all the rest of the month, but now they become deadly serious and she gets the feeling that they're hopeless. There's a common name for this condition. It's called premenstrual tension. Usually depression and the bloated feeling, which actually is caused by the retention of a great deal of water in the system, disappear as suddenly as they came. Several medical preparations are on the market to relieve premenstrual tension.

If a girl has periods of depression or moodiness that come and go, she might be wise to mark off a calendar to tell her just when she was feeling low and when she felt on top of the world. If she keeps this calendar for a few months, and also notes when her menstrual period began, she may see that there's a definite pattern of depression before the cycle begins or during the middle period. And if she realizes that these feelings of depression or even despair are the result of physical factors and will disappear within a few days, she'll be able to adjust to them better. She'll realize that they'll pass, and that the world will then seem a much better place again.

MENSTRUATION. Under *Growing Up*, See *Changes in girls*.

MISCARRIAGE. This is what happens when a baby is born before he's old enough to live outside his mother's body. We don't know all the reasons for miscarriages, but we do know that a baby must be in his mother's body six months at the very least before he's well enough developed to live outside of it.

Miscarriages sometimes happen when the baby isn't growing right or if his mother has been very sick or hurt in some way. Doctors sometimes use the term abortion when speaking of miscarriage, but this isn't the abortion which is a sin unless the mother deliberately does something to harm her baby. Miscarriage is a spontaneous abortion. The abortion which is a grievous mortal sin is induced abortion, or deliberate abortion.

MODESTY. If you had valuable land you wanted to protect from outsiders, you'd build a high fence so that no intruders could get in without your knowledge. Your virtue is your most prized possession, and it's also necessary to protect it from despoilers. You have to build a fence around it, too—a fence which goes by the name of modesty.

Modesty is the protector of virtue. Almost without fail, you'll find that a person who commits impurity has first been immodest in things he said or did. Only after the wall of modesty has been surmounted is it possible to trample on virtue.

That's why parents and teachers want boys and girls to be modest in their appearance, conduct and conversation. You're being modest when you wear modest clothing, when you don't use profane or immodest talk, don't think it's smart to wisecrack about sex, and make sure you don't get involved in necking sessions which could quickly get out of hand. When you have a sense of protectiveness about your body and refuse to let it be anyone's plaything, you're acting modestly and keeping up high the fence that protects your purity.

Whenever you're tempted to act or speak immodestly, just remember that your modesty is morality's first line of defense and that if this goes, it will be that much easier to lose your virtue and innocence as well.

MORNING SICKNESS. Some women in the early stages of pregnancy experience a kind of nausea when they wake up, or soon afterwards.

NATURAL CHILDBIRTH. This is a way of giving birth in which the use of drugs is avoided as much as possible. This method of childbirth was developed when it was realized that many modern mothers don't get as much exercise and develop their muscles as much as women who did more hard physical labor around the home and in the fields. These modern mothers sometimes have a difficult time because they use muscles in the physical labor of giving birth that they don't use any other time. So giving birth is harder on these women than it is on somebody whose muscles are better developed.

Mothers who use the natural childbirth method take exercise during pregnancy so that they'll have an easier time during labor. It's almost like somebody practicing tennis or basketball or any other sport for a big game that's coming up. The mothers also learn special breathing methods so they can endure labor pains better.

An advantage of natural childbirth is that mothers often don't need relief from pain during their delivery. They're able to stay awake and see what's going on while the

baby's being born. There are many people who think
natural childbirth is the best method.

NECKING.   See *Kissing, Petting*.

NEWSPAPERS.   See *Reading Matter*.

NOCTURNAL EMISSIONS.   Discharge of semen by boys and
   men in their sleep. Under *Growing Up,* See *Changes
   in boys.*

NUDITY.   God gave each one of us our bodies, and He
   made all of our organs for a definite purpose. We use
   our hands to reach for things and hold them. We use
   our mouths to eat and to speak, we use our eyes to
   see. We use our sex organs to dispose of some of the
   waste matter from our bodies, all according to God's
   plan.

   Now, since God could never make anything evil, we
should never be ashamed of our bodies or to think there
is anything sinful or dirty about them. Anything that God
gives us is good if we use it the way He wants us to.

   Because He wants us to use our sex organs only in a
special and private way, and because they serve a very
sacred purpose in bringing babies into the world, we should
keep them very special and sacred. We do this by keeping
those parts of our body covered because we don't want
them to be seen by other people.

OBSTETRICIAN.   He's a doctor who specializes in taking
   care of women who are going to have babies, and in
   delivering the babies when they're born.

   Years ago, most mothers had their babies at home and
were lucky if they had even a trained nurse to help them.
Millions of babies were born safely that way, but often the
babies and their mothers died because they didn't have
good medical care. If a woman goes to an obstetrician as
soon as she realizes that she's going to have a baby, and

does what he tells her, she has a much better chance of having a healthy baby and of being safe herself.

OVARIES. These are the organs in the woman's body which store the eggs which could be fertilized and grow into babies.

PARENTHOOD—REQUIREMENTS FOR. When boys and girls reach the age of fourteen or fifteen, they usually have the physical ability to become fathers and mothers. But they still have a long way to go before they're ready to bring a baby into the world. You can understand this if you realize all the things a parent has to do for a baby.

First of all, a mother must spend almost all of her time taking care of a new baby. When a child is born, he must be fed every four hours or so, his clothes must be changed regularly, he must be given baths and fresh air, and he must be watched over carefully to make sure he doesn't get sick. For at least a couple of years, before he learns to walk and talk, his mother must be near him almost all the time. Even when he's asleep, somebody must be near to take care of him if he wakes up crying. It would be a terrible thing, for example, if his parents went out at night and left him alone at home and the house caught fire.

Then while the baby's at school, his mother has to spend many hours every day taking care of him—making his meals, cleaning up after him, washing and mending his clothing, making sure he does his homework, and making sure he eats the right things and keeps in good health. All this takes time, and it goes on until he's old enough to care for himself.

While a mother's doing this, the father has his work cut out for him too. It's his job to provide for his family —to earn the money to buy food and clothing, pay for where the family lives, the heat and all the other things that the family needs. He and his wife probably will also have to try to save money to help their child get a good education. This means parents often must do without things they'd like to have. Maybe they'd like new clothing for themselves, new furniture for the living room, a new car, a trip on their vacation or lots of other things. They don't get them because they need the money for their children.

Being a mother or father involves even more than that. Parents have a responsibility to help their child form his soul properly. They have to try to help him to lead a good life so he can grow up as a good man or woman. That means they have to give a good example. They have to remember that when they die God will ask them what they did with the baby He gave them, and this is a responsibility no parent should take lightly.

Of course, this shouldn't make you think being a mother or father is an impossible job. It's not—not if you have God's help. Because a mother and father are doing God's work, they know they can ask for His help whenever they need it. So being a parent isn't really so difficult with God's help as it would be without it.

Why bring up the problems a parent has? Just because every young person should realize that having a child doesn't end with the delivery of the baby in the hospital. It goes on for eighteen years or even longer. And that means that before boys and girls should think of getting married, they should make sure they're grown up enough to take on all the responsibilities they'll have to face.

When you consider all that's involved in being a parent, I think you'll agree that it's not a job for babies. The older and more mature you are, the better education you have, and the greater sense of responsibility you have, the more likely it is that you'll do a good job as a parent. But as a rule a young person just doesn't have the training, experience or maturity to do these things. That's why almost everybody who's had any experience with parenthood—mothers and fathers themselves, the Church, teachers, doctors, and everybody else—strongly suggests that young people wait until they're at least out of their teens before they take on these responsibilities.

PENIS. The male sex organ. Urine is passed through it, and also the sperm in the act of intercourse.

PETTING. An old saying describes the difference between necking and petting: Necking is what happens from the neck up, and petting is what happens from the neck down.

For any unmarried person, petting is wrong. Period. It's wrong because it has no other purpose but to stir up sex passions, and can't help but put a lot of ideas in petters' minds that don't belong there.

Petting is not only a sin, it's also dangerous. It's dangerous because it can get out of hand more easily than you think, and before long, the persons involved find they can't stop themselves from going all the way. People who run homes for unwed mothers, or who deal with girls who are forced to marry whether they want to or not, say that almost without exception, the whole trouble started with petting that got beyond control. The way to stay out of trouble is to know what's dangerous—and to recognize the danger signs that lead to it. You can be sure that the biggest danger sign pointing to sin and unwanted pregnancies is having a boy or girl friend who's interested in petting as a way of life and thinks it's all good, harmless fun.

PLACENTA. See *Afterbirth*.

POSTNATAL CARE. Also known as after-care or postpartum

care. This is the care given by a doctor or nurse to a mother after her baby is born.

PREGNANCY. The condition of a woman who is going to have a baby. See *Prenatal Care, Babies.*

PREMATURE BABY. A baby is called premature if he's born more than two weeks earlier than the average of nine months that babies take to develop in their mother's bodies, or if he weighs less than five and a half pounds at birth. Many of these babies don't have enough fat on their bodies yet to keep them warm, so they're placed in special heated cribs called incubators until they're big and strong enough to live in regular cribs, the way babies born at the regular time do.

PRENATAL CARE. This term describes the special attention a mother-to-be needs when she's expecting a baby. Generally, it's always a good idea for a mother to go to a doctor as soon as she thinks she may be pregnant, and to follow the exact advice he gives her.

Most women may have some discomfort while they're expecting a baby—things like heartburn, indigestion, trouble sleeping and the like—but if a mother cares for herself properly when she's carrying a baby and does what her doctor tells her, she probably won't have any lasting ill effects.

The doctor may give her a special diet so she won't get too fat, may prescribe special medicines, and may tell her she needs to take naps during the day or to get extra rest at night, and so on.

PRIVACY. Everybody has a right to be alone by himself when he's doing certain things like getting undressed, going to the toilet, taking a bath, and so on. Of course, tiny children can't do those things themselves and their mothers and fathers have to help them, but when they become old enough they should have privacy, too. They should close the bathroom door, for example, so that nobody sees them when they're on the toilet.

Brothers and sisters and mothers and fathers have rights to privacy too. That means that if Mother is in the bathroom, you shouldn't burst in on her, but should always knock on the door first to make sure it's all right to come in. Before you enter another person's bedroom where the door is closed, you should knock and wait until the person tells you to come in.

If you want your privacy, so you're able to be alone without having other people burst in on you, you have to respect other people's privacy too.

PROSTITUTE. A person who performs the sex act for money.

PUBERTY. This is a word we use to describe the condition when a girl acquires the physical characteristics of a woman, and a boy acquires the powers of a man. A girl who has reached the age of puberty has begun to menstruate, because menstruation is a sign that her ovaries have begun to discharge the eggs which could be fertilized and make her a mother. Boys know they have reached this age when they wake up sometimes and discover that they have discharged a fluid in their sleep. This fluid contains sperm which could fertilize an egg in a woman's body and result in a baby.

There are other signs that show that the age of puberty is at hand. These include the enlargement of breasts and the growth of hair around the sex organs in girls and the growth of the penis and testicles and an increase in hair around the sex organs of boys.

PUBIC AREA. The part of the body around the sex organs which is covered by hair when a child becomes an adolescent. Hair in this region is known as pubic hair.

RAPE. This describes what happens when a man forces a woman to have intercourse against her wishes. It is also called criminal assault. It is a very serious crime, and a man who commits it can go to jail for a long period of time.

READING MATTER. You've heard the expression "The pen is mightier than the sword." There's a great deal of truth in that saying. It means that books can change people's minds and can move them to do things by the power of persuasion that no amount of force could accomplish. Good reading matter is one of the great pleasures in life. Books, magazines and newspapers can provide a great deal of satisfaction and can help you lead a happier life in every respect. But bad reading matter can cause you a great deal of harm.

As you've probably noticed, many books and magazines are written and published with no other purpose but to arouse sexual desires, to get you all stirred up and to get you to think sinful thoughts. Your soul can be poisoned by this kind of material just as surely as your body can be poisoned by a dose of arsenic. Maybe you won't feel the effects of the poison on your soul at first. You can take tiny amounts of poison without feeling any effect, but if you repeat these doses the poison keeps building up in your system. Eventually it will kill you just as surely as if you had taken it all in one dose.

As you know, passion is a very powerful thing. It can start into motion as a result of very simple stimulation. That's why it's so important to keep away from reading matter that could stir you up.

This is another case where it's important to know yourself. Better than anyone else, you know how you react to certain things you see in print. You know whether they leave you cold and indifferent, or whether they get you thinking along lines you know are wrong.

Of course, there are plenty of examples of reading matter that's wrong for almost everybody. These are the magazines and books that have no other purpose but to pander to the lowest human instincts. But many other publications might be put on the borderline. They might be an occasion of temptation for some people, but not for others. These are the ones you have to consider for yourself, knowing your own reactions. If they're bad for you, you should avoid them even if they don't have the same effect on other people.

RECTUM. The lower end of the bowels through which waste matter from the body passes.

RELIGIOUS LIFE. It's true that a great number of people grow up and get married, and it's possible that you will too. But it's a mistake to think marriage is the only vocation for a man or woman.

God may call you to a different state in life. He may want you to devote your life to His service as a priest, brother or nun. If so, this is a wonderful opportunity you're being offered—a chance to do a magnificent work in the world, to bring God's message to the young and old, to comfort the sick and people who have deep sorrow, to help the poor and the downtrodden. When you help your fellow man, you're doing God's work, and this is the most satisfying kind of life you can lead. It's the kind of work God has in mind for all mankind, because we are all brothers in His human family.

There are any number of satisfactions that come from the religious life. One of the greatest is the satisfaction of knowing that you're in the best possible position to serve God completely. When you lead the life of a religious, you're in constant touch with Him.

A religious must lead a life of celibacy. That means you can't marry or have children. This is a great sacrifice, of course, but it's a sacrifice millions of people have been able to make happily, because while they give up some of the pleasures of life that other people have in raising a family, they also have a greater sense of satisfaction in the work they do and the knowledge that they're of real service to God and their fellow man.

Sometimes it's not easy to tell if you have a vocation. But if you're in a good spiritual state, have good health and a desire to do something especially worthwhile with your life, it's at least possible that God wants you to work for Him directly. Think about it and pray that you learn exactly what life He wants you to follow.

The important thing is to keep your mind open to the possibility of the religious life. Don't think you *have* to marry to lead a happy life. You may be more at home as a religious than in any other vocation.

REPRODUCTION. This word describes God's plan which enables all living things—human beings, animals and plants—to come into being. A father and mother engage in reproduction when they have a baby, and God has seen to it that all the animals have ways to bring baby animals into the world. He also has arranged it so that a plant produces seed which is scattered on the ground and grows into new plants.

RH BABIES. Most people have a chemical in their blood containing what is known as the Rh factor. People who don't have this substance are called Rh negative. As far as we know, whether you have this substance in your blood doesn't make any difference in how you look or your health.

The only time it seems to make a difference is when a father has this Rh factor in his blood and the mother doesn't have it. There is seldom any danger to the first child of such parents, but some danger to the lives of subsequent fetuses.

Obstetricians, the doctors who take care of mothers who are going to have babies, know all about these dangers. They make blood tests as a matter of course. If they have to, they will give the baby blood transfusions as soon as he is born, to make sure that nothing will happen to him.

When the Rh factor exists, which is only about one time in two hundred births, the baby is often referred to as an Rh baby. But after he's born safely, he's just as healthy as any other baby.

RHYTHM METHOD. The natural way of limiting birth, which is permitted by the Church. It involves a knowledge of a woman's menstrual rhythm and the fact that there are only certain days in each month (around the middle of the menstrual cycle) when she could have a baby if she had intercourse. See *Family Limitation* and *Contraception*.

SATYR. A man obsessed with the idea of satisfying his sexual impulses at every possible opportunity.

SCROTUM. The bag which hangs beneath the penis and contains the testes.

SCRUPULOSITY. You've probably heard the expression "He's unscrupulous." It means this person has no scruples—he won't let his conscience bother him about anything. He'll lie, cheat, steal, and violate all the Commandments without giving a thought to the fact that he's going directly against the will of God.

The opposite of the unscrupulous person is the scrupulous one. The unscrupulous man does sinful things and thinks they're natural and ordinary—nothing to worry about. The scrupulous person, on the other hand, does natural and ordinary things that are nothing to worry about—but thinks they're sinful.

Some people are so scrupulous that they think every

little thought that comes to them is a sin. A girl who went to Confession, then came home and looked at a newspaper picture of a handsome man that made her think of sex for a few fleeting seconds, would certainly be way off base if she decided she wasn't worthy to receive the Blessed Sacrament the next day. She'd be too scrupulous. She should realize that as long as she didn't encourage the thought and dwell on it once she realized what it was, she did all that was expected of her.

Remember that you're not responsible for every thought that enters your mind. Thoughts of sex are natural, and it's natural to have some curiosity about it. But while you're not responsible for tempting and disturbing thoughts that come into your mind, you must try to get rid of them if you can. Sometimes they don't go away easily and may linger despite your best efforts.

If you do nothing to encourage sex thoughts, you're not responsible for them. God knows that you're trying to do the right thing. He doesn't blame you if you try to get rid of the temptation, even if you don't seem to be able to.

Also remember that there's a big difference between a venial sin and a mortal sin, and that all sins are not equally bad. If they were, probably few people could stay in the state of grace for long. When you commit little sins, you should be sorry for them, of course, and you should resolve to avoid them in the future. But because you committed a little sin doesn't mean that you're contemptible in the eyes of God. You should realize that you've done wrong, but not enough to keep you from Holy Communion.

If you deliberately dwelt on immoral or impure thoughts and took a great deal of pleasure from them, that would be an entirely different matter. Then you would have committed a grievous sin.

To avoid both extremes—the extreme of not caring at

all about what you do, and the extreme of scrupulosity or worrying too much about every little thing that happens —you should follow a middle course. You should realize that God is a loving Father Who has set down rules for you. He will not overlook big sins but He is not such a tyrant that you have to feel He'll condemn you to hell-fire because of some little offense you've committed. He does not expect the impossible. If you try to do a reasonably good job, you can be sure that He will not look with disfavor upon you.

SEDUCTION. This word is defined in the dictionary as the act of persuading somebody to do something wrong. It usually means to persuade someone to engage in a sinful act against the Sixth Commandment.

For girls. The act of seduction may be something that happens on the spur of the moment, but more often it's something that may be carried out over a period of time— even for weeks or months. It's important for you to realize that seduction can take many different forms. If you learn to recognize what these forms are, you'll be better able to defend yourself against them before it's too late.

One of the most common signs that an attempted seduction may be in the making is when a boy or man starts paying you attention far beyond anything that might reasonably be expected. For example, it may be customary for a boy to take a girl to a movie and to have a soda or snack afterwards. If he went all out and started giving the girl expensive presents, she should rightly wonder what's in the back of his mind. If the boy is a great deal older than she is and gives the impression that he's had some experience with sex and also starts showering her with gifts, she can be almost sure that his intentions aren't all they should be.

It's normal for a boy to pay some compliments to a girl, to tell her how pretty she is, what an agreeable personality she has and so on. It's even customary to lay it on a little bit. But if he starts laying on the flattery with a trowel, and starts handing out compliments that you yourself know are exaggerations, you ought to be suspicious.

A boy who has sin in the back of his mind generally tips off his intentions long before the actual attempt at seduction begins. One way is to ply a girl with drinks so she won't know what she's doing, or at least so that her defenses will be down when he tries to have relations with her. Watch out for the boy who tries to create a situation where he will be all alone with you with nobody to interrupt him. That's why when a boy parks his car in a secluded spot, a girl is right to suspect that he's up to no good.

One of the most dangerous signs of all is when a male arranges matters so that he and a girl are alone in a house or apartment for a long period of time. A boy may wait until his parents go out for the evening, and no one else is at home, to invite a girl friend over. Or he may get himself invited to the girl's house when her parents are away, or to where she may be baby-sitting for the evening.

If you use ordinary common sense, you usually can detect would-be seducers. As a general rule, they're anybody you ordinarily wouldn't expect to be interested in you—like a man much older than you or a boy whose interests are entirely different from your own. This is another way of saying that the person to beware of especially is one you know you wouldn't have a chance of marrying. Once you recognize this type of person, don't give him the time of day and keep as far away from him as you can.

For boys. It used to be that almost all the seducers in the world were men. Like many other things, that has changed quite a bit in the past fifty years or so. Now it often happens that a female will set out to trap a male and cause him to have intercourse with her.

The seducers of boys and young men are often women much older than themselves. It's certainly not wrong for you to be friendly with an older woman, but if she starts getting too friendly—giving you gifts for no good reason, for instance—it's time to wonder what she has in mind.

You may also encounter girls your own age, and maybe even younger than you, who have absolutely no moral scruples and even stoop to stirring you up deliberately. Watch out for the girl who's ready to neck at the drop of a hat—and also for the one who seems to be trying to create situations where you'll be alone with her for a long period of time.

Some boys are all too eager to become involved with such people, but the results aren't always what they expect. In the first place, there's always the serious danger of disease, because a girl who has found out what sex is all about and who's ready, willing and eager to engage in it with anybody who comes along is a likely candidate for venereal disease, which she can easily give to everybody she has relations with. And it happens more often than most people realize that the girl turns up later with the announcement that she's pregnant and that the boy had better marry her or else.

SEMEN. The fluid which contains the male sperm. It is also called seminal fluid.

SEX DIFFERENCES. God made men and women different because He wants them to do different kinds of jobs. He gives a woman a soft body, broad hips, and a long abdomen so she'll be able to carry a baby inside her for the nine months it takes him to grow big enough to be born. He gives her large breasts so she can feed her baby until he's strong enough to eat other foods.

God made men to be fathers and do the heavy work that must be done to take care of mothers and babies. That's why men usually have stronger bodies and bigger shoulders and muscles.

God makes men and women different in many other ways. Women are usually more emotional so they'll be better able to take care of their children, to comfort them and sympathize with them, when they are ill. Men are made stronger so they can go out and work in the world. God makes a mother to be the heart of the family, and makes a father to be the head.

SEX STIMULATION. Both boys and girls on a date must always realize that they have a definite responsibility to avoid words or deeds that would create sexual desire in their companion.

Girls sometimes don't realize that boys are quick on the trigger when it comes to sex. What to a girl might be a kiss that doesn't stimulate her in any way may get a boy aroused to such an extent that he finds it difficult to control his sexual impulses. Another thing that could set a boy off is clothing that shows too much of the body. Many a girl who thinks she's just wearing the latest style would be shocked to realize that boys looking at her think only of sex.

Boys also should realize that they're much more likely to get worked up than girls are. They should keep away from any situation that's likely to create thoughts they shouldn't have.

SEX TALK. There's nothing wrong in talking about sex with your friends if your purpose is to get honest information or honest attitudes. Your friends may have read or heard things and may be able to give you a clearer picture of some aspect of sex than you've been able to get in any other way. But you ought to remember that information you pick up from friends is likely to be wrong at least part of the time. Boys and girls often pick up so-called facts that are completely false and may even worry that they're not developing as they should.

If you have any questions about sex, never be ashamed to ask your parents about it. We don't know all the answers but we can probably tell what's true and what isn't. And you can get plenty of books which tell everything you want to know in a reverent manner.

It's wrong to discuss sex in a flippant way, as though it's something dirty. Since God made sex to serve the sacred purpose of bringing babies into the world, it should never be made obscene. That's why dirty stories and dirty words used to describe the sex organs and sex acts are always out of order. When people talk about the subject in such a way that they get some kind of secret enjoyment out of it, they offend God because they turn something He made from a holy thing into an ugly one.

SODOMY. Perverted sexual intercourse which is often engaged in by homosexuals. It also covers a sexual act between a man and woman which is not completed in the normal manner. The word comes from the ancient city of Sodom, which God destroyed for its sin.

SPERM. This is a shortened word which means the same as spermatozoön. It is the male sex cell of reproduction. When it unites with an ovum, the egg cell of a female, a new life begins.

SOUL KISSING. Also called tongue kissing, this has sexual stimulation as its only purpose. It is wrong for the unmarried, and dangerous for the same reason that petting is dangerous.

STERILE PERIOD. That time of the month, generally (but not always) preceding and just following menstruation, when a woman cannot become pregnant. Conception, or the beginning of pregnancy, is possible only in the few days before, during, and after ovulation around the middle of the cycle, when an egg is discharged from the ovary and moves through the Fallopian tubes to the uterus.

STERILIZATION. This is an operation a man or woman deliberately has so that he or she won't be able to become a father or mother. The operation of the male involves cutting the duct which carries sperm out of the body, making it impossible for the sperm to be discharged. Sperm is needed to unite with an egg cell in the female if a baby is to be conceived.

In a woman, the operation involves cutting off or bypassing the Fallopian tubes which eggs pass through on the way from the ovaries to the uterus. If the eggs cannot get past the tubes, they cannot be fertilized and the woman cannot become a mother.

Any operation that deliberately mutilates an organ without a good reason is a sin. It would be a sin, for example, to cut off your hands or ears.

Another reason sterilization is wrong is that it deliberately tries to avoid the function for which God gave men and women their sex organs. He gave them these organs so they could become fathers and mothers. To use the organs in a way He did not intend obviously violates His plan for us.

People who allow this operation to be performed often live to regret it. Once the operation is done, it's usually permanent and the person cannot have another operation later to make things the way they were originally. Sometimes people think they don't want children. A few years later, they want them. But then it's too late. They can't do anything about it. And the thought that they've deliberately destroyed a function of their own bodies is something that will bother their consciences until they die.

SYPHILIS. A disease people get by having intercourse with a person already affected, or by other very close contacts. See *Venereal Disease*.

TEMPTATIONS. Everybody has them, and everybody has to learn how to handle them. Every day of our lives, we meet temptations to do things that are not best for us and it's important that we get into the habit while we're young of saying No to them.

When you wake up in the morning and see that it's time to get ready for school, you may be tempted to go back to sleep. Unless you resist that temptation, you'll miss your class and will be punished in some way as a result. If you have homework at night, you may be tempted to look at a television program, but unless you resist the temptation you'll get a poor mark and may even fail the course.

We have to say No to the temptation to abuse every power that God has given us, not just the power of sex. For example, we have the power to speak—but that doesn't mean we should say mean things that would hurt other people. God gives us the power to enjoy food, but if we didn't control the temptation to eat too much we'd get sick.

Just because God gives you sexual organs doesn't mean you can use them any way you want. You are to use them only when you are married and can become a parent. The rest of the time, you must learn to say No to temptations to use them in any other way.

The power of passion is very strong, and sometimes temptations will be very strong too. Try to think of other things. Or do something to take your mind off the subject. Take a walk, play a game, mow the lawn, wash your face —if you do something active, you generally will start thinking about what you're doing and the temptation will pass away.

TESTES. The male organs which are in the scrotum, the bag that hangs beneath the penis. The testes produce sperm as well as certain hormones. They are also called testicles.

TOILET, PUBLIC. There's a danger of getting a disease from somebody who just used the same toilet, drinking glass or towel as you. For this reason, always be careful when you use a toilet that's used by a great number of people you don't know. Toilet seats may contain germs, so it's wise to cover the seat with toilet paper.

Try to avoid using a towel in a public toilet that has been used by somebody else. It's probably loaded with germs. It's all right to use a rolling towel, when you press a button and get a clean piece of it for yourself. Of course, it's also all right to use a paper towel which you get fresh and can then throw away. Some places have machines that blow warm air on your hands to dry them after you wash yourself. These are safe too.

Don't drink from a cup or glass that has been used by another person unless it has been washed thoroughly in hot water. If you use a drinking fountain where the water comes from a spout, make sure that your mouth doesn't touch the spout itself.

Most disease germs are passed from person to person, either by direct contact or by using the same thing and enabling germs to get in the mouth. Always remember this and take precautions to protect yourself.

Never use a public toilet in an out-of-the-way place, where there aren't several other people around. The reason is that sick men and women sometimes bother boys and girls in public toilets, and may even try to harm them. If any stranger starts talking to you about your private organs or gets very personal with you in a public toilet, leave at once and go where there are people around who could help you if the person continues to bother you.

Twins. Sometimes the single egg cell of the mother which is the beginning of a baby turns into two or more cells after it has been fertilized. These separate cells in the mother's body start developing by themselves, so that instead of having one baby growing inside her, she has two, three or even more. These babies who start from the same cell are called identical twins. They're both either boys or girls, because the one cell they started from can be only that of a boy or a girl. Identical twins always look alike, but are likely to be mirror images of each other. One will usually be left-handed, the other right-handed; one will part his hair on the left, the other on the right, etc. Sometimes it's impossible for people outside the family to tell them apart.

There are other kinds of twins who don't look alike and who may be of different sexes. Sometimes twins are very different. These twins are called fraternal twins. They're the result of two cells of the mother being fertilized by different sperm from the father at about the same time. These different fertilized eggs grow in the mother's body like separate babies.

Umbilical cord. This is a thick cord, almost like rope, which connects the baby in the womb to the placenta, or wall of the mother's uterus. In this cord are blood vessels that carry nourishment and oxygen from the mother to the baby and also carry away from the baby's body all the waste matter. When the baby is born, the doctor cuts the umbilical cord because the baby can now breathe, take in food and get rid of waste matter all by himself. The place where the umbilical cord was cut is at the navel, or belly button.

URETHRA.   Everybody has a tube which carries urine from the bladder to outside the body. In the male, it is also the passage semen passes through before it is discharged.

URINE.   The liquid discharged from our bodies when we go to the toilet.

URINALYSIS.   By testing the urine we pass from our bodies, scientists can tell what it consists of—various chemicals, how much sugar, and other factors. In this way, they can also detect certain diseases which might be difficult to find in any other way. For example, a urinalysis can indicate whether a person has diabetes by the amount of sugar it contains. Because there are many changes in a mother's body when she becomes pregnant, scientists are trying to perfect a urine test that would tell with certainty whether she's going to have a baby or not, long before any other signs show up.

UTERUS.   Also known as the womb, this is the organ in the mother where a baby stays and grows during pregnancy.

VAGINA.   The sex organ of girls and women that begins just inside the body and leads to the neck of the uterus. It's through the vagina that the baby travels when it is being born, and it's also through the vagina that the father's sperm travels on the way to penetrate the egg of the mother.

VENEREAL DISEASE.   This is a disease which can be spread by one person to another when their bodies come into close contact, as, for example, when they kiss very emotionally or have sexual relations. The common venereal diseases go by the names of syphilis and gonorrhea. These diseases can be very serious and can cause lasting damage. If syphilis isn't treated in time, it can cause blindness, insanity and death.

At one time there was no real cure for these venereal diseases at all. New drugs and treatment have been developed which now make it possible to control them if treatment is begun in time. But even today many cases are extremely difficult to cure. Apparently new strains of germs carrying the diseases have been developed that resist the so-called miracle drugs. As a result, there has been a continuous, steady increase in recent years in the number of persons getting these diseases.

Since it's rare for a person to contract a venereal disease in any way but by sexual activity, it stands to reason that the best defense against them is to avoid intercourse outside of marriage. The person who doesn't do this runs a real risk of contracting these diseases, as well as committing a mortal sin and maybe being responsible for bringing an innocent baby into the world.

VIRGIN. A virgin is someone who has never had sexual relations with the opposite sex. Virgins have always held a special place in history, and the Church has always honored those who remain virgins because of their love of God.

The greatest virgin, of course, was the Blessed Virgin, Mother of Our Lord. She remained a virgin all her life and this is what is remarkable about her. Everyone else in the world has been born as a result of the seed from a man uniting with the seed of a woman in the woman's body. But the Blessed Virgin never had this relationship with her husband, Saint Joseph. Instead, Mary was "conceived of the Holy Ghost" and had her baby, Jesus, in a way that was entirely special and different.

VULVA. The outside part of the female sex organs. The folds of skin that surround the opening to the vagina and the urethra.

WET DREAMS. These are dreams which boys and men have

232) YOUR CHILD AND SEX

and which are accompanied by a discharge of semen. Under *Growing Up*, see *Changes in boys*.

WOMB.   Another word for the uterus.

WORDS, DIRTY.   Almost everything you can mention has a good purpose, but you can turn it into a bad purpose by using it the wrong way. For example, matches are very important in helping us start a fire so we can cook food or keep warm in the wintertime. But it would be wrong to use matches to burn the house down.

It's the same with our power to speak. God gives us this power so we can talk to each other. You can talk and ask for food if you're hungry, you can tell me if you don't feel well, you can sing songs and tell jokes—all because you can use words. When you do those things you are using your power to speak in the right way. But there also is a bad way to use your power to speak, and that is by using words you should not use.

Sometimes these words are not nice. We don't use them because using them would be like picking your nose in public.

Other words are even worse to use. These are vulgar words that deal with subjects that should not be talked about in a vulgar way. Having babies should never be talked about with such words, because God has made this a sacred subject.

Some words are sins to use because they use the name of God in vain. If you use the name of God or Jesus or the Blessed Mother or the Saints, it should always be in a very special way, with complete reverence. God is all good. We should never use His name in a way that could offend Him.

Index

About the Author

Monsignor Kelly, now Director of the Family Life Bureau of the Archdiocese of New York, was ordained at St. Patrick's Cathedral in New York City in 1942. For three years thereafter he studied at the Catholic University of America, obtaining his Ph.D. degree in Social Science in 1946. He was Assistant Pastor at St. Monica's Church in New York City from 1945 to 1956, and is now Assistant Pastor at Sacred Heart Church, New York City. From 1946 through 1949, Father Kelly lectured at St. Joseph's Seminary, and in 1952 he was a lecturer at the Catholic University of America.

A member of the American Catholic Historical Association, Monsignor Kelly is the author of *The Catholic Marriage Manual, The Catholic Family Handbook, The Catholic Youth's Guide to Life and Love* as well as *Your Child and Sex: A Guide for Catholic Parents.* He also wrote *Catholics and the Practice of the Faith, Primer on the Taft-Hartley Law* and *History of St. Monica's Parish.*